8.95

To Dr. P. Yeu
with deep gratitude
Charlie

MW01380118

The Holy Dybbuk

Letters of Charles Rich, Contemplative

edited by Ronda Chervin

ST. BEDE'S PUBLICATIONS
Petersham, Massachusetts

Copyright © 1988 by Ronda Chervin
All Rights Reserved
PRINTED IN THE UNITED STATES OF AMERICA
4   3   2

Imprimatur: +Timothy J. Harrington
Bishop of Worcester
January 12, 1988

The *Imprimatur* is an official declaration that a book is considered to be free of doctrinal and moral error. It is not implied that those who have granted the *Imprimatur* necessarily agree with the contents, opinions or statements expressed.

Cover design by Basil Atwell, OSB
Monk of Assumption Abbey

LIBRARY OF CONGRESS CATALOGING IN PUBLICATION DATA

Rich, Charles.
   The holy dybbuk.

   1. Rich, Charles—Correspondence.   2. Catholics—United States—Correspondence.   3. Converts from Judaism—Correspondence.
4. Chervin, Ronda—Correspondence.   I. Chervin, Ronda.
II. Title.
BX4705.R458A3   1987   282'.092'4   [B]   87-16663
ISBN 0-932506-50-X

Published by St. Bede's Publications
P.O. Box 545
Petersham, Massachusetts 01366-0545

Introduction

Twenty-seven years ago, right after my conversion to the Catholic faith from an atheistic Jewish background, I had the joy of meeting a giant of the Faith. A lay contemplative, then in his sixties, Charles Rich had been living in a Jesuit community as a guest for many years. He was also a Jewish convert, but from an orthodox family.

I was immediately attracted to Charlie (as he is always called) by the fiery mystical ardor of his love of Christ. He is my closest friend and yet we rarely see each other. He has always resided in New York and I have been in Rome, Spring Valley, Capistrano, Los Angeles, and many other places during the period between 1960-1984. Being a married woman with three children and a career as a philosophy professor, a speaker, and writer, my life pattern diverged exceedingly from the profound inwardness of the daily experience of Charlie Rich. Nonetheless, the bond of spiritual friendship was never broken. The nature of the tie was never based on visits, projects, or even natural affinity, but rather on a mysterious grace-filled unity of spirit. The letters, which are excerpted in this volume, grew in frequency from being a delightful break from the busyness of my very full life, into a daily correspondence—a journal of the interior experience of God shared between us.

So that you may have a more vivid image of the author of these letters, here is a short biographical sketch. A longer one can be found in my introduction to Charlie's book, *The Embrace of the Soul: Meditations on the Song of Songs*, published by St. Bede's in 1984.

Born in the mountains of Hungary in 1899, Charlie, called Chaskel, was raised in an orthodox environment not unlike the town of Anatevke immortalized in *Fiddler on the Roof*. At an early age his desire for prayer set him apart from his brother and sisters, giving him exemption from menial chores as he pursued studies and roamed in the forest in rapt contemplation of God.

A violent change took place, in a life which would have led to the rabbinate, when the family moved to New York City. Dire poverty led his father to insist that the children go to work as soon as possible. And *iv* / *Introduction*

so, with but three years of formal school in the English language, Charlie found himself in the world of the sweatshops of the Jewish ghetto.

Although his mother was a saintly Jewess of a Chasidic lineage—a spirituality emphasizing joy in God—and his father was a pious but more legalistic Jew, the young son lost his faith. Immersed in city life, without the beauty of nature and the solitude of the forest, God became a distant object with whom his soul could find no means of communion.

Yet, a mind as profound as Charlie's could not remain content with the rounds of his work. While earning his keep as a waiter, he began to attend the free lectures given at Cooper Union in New York City. A former school teacher, an atheist, took the young man in hand and tutored him until he was able to read all the classics he could get his hands on at the 42nd Street library.

But many years of study failed to bring Charlie the wisdom he was seeking. At the age of thirty-three, completely discouraged, he tried twice to commit suicide. Unable to succeed even in the elimination of himself, he was trudging through the streets one day when he came upon an old Neo-Gothic Catholic church. Entering merely in order to cool down, he sat in a pew and lifted his eyes to a stained glass window depicting the apostles in a storm and the luminous figure of Christ commanding them to have faith. Abruptly, the words came to Charlie from the Christ in the window, "I am God."

This was the beginning of a conversion so complete that soon Charlie was praying in a semi-trance for twelve hours a day. Once a Catholic, he tried to enter various monastic orders, but his absorption in prayer made any kind of labor impossible, and it was finally decided that his vocation would be to live in the world as a lay contemplative, eventually as a guest of the Jesuit order from whose ranks he has always taken his spiritual director.

It is harder to describe the physical appearance of one known and loved for many years than that of a new acquaintance. When I first met Charlie in his early sixties, he was short and lean, though strong, with a long face marked by lines not only of mental suffering but also coming from years of destitution in the past. At the same time, his fiery black

Introduction / *v*

eyes were always sparkling with humor so that he never gave a melancholy impression when animated in conversation. His strong Yiddish accent and vehement manner of speech always gave his friends the feeling of being with a remarkable character as well as a wonderful saint.

Now, at eighty-eight, his features have mellowed. His face is rounder, and his expression gets progressively sweeter as he nears his longed-for goal: eternity.

A word about the title: *The Holy Dybbuk*. One of the most popular and greatest Jewish plays is called *The Dybbuk*. Written by Rappaport, originally in Yiddish, the story involves a poverty-stricken Chasidic scholar, Chanon, of the sort depicted in the movies *Fiddler on the Roof* and *Yentl*.

Tired of the legalism of his Talmudic studies, Chanon begins to dabble in the forbidden books of the Cabbala. At this time, he falls in love with a beautiful young girl, Leah, who is engaged to be married to a suitor chosen by her parents.

In an agony of grief and jealously, Chanon tries the lore of the Cabbala to wrest the girl away from her betrothed. But when he speaks the magic words, he falls dead on the floor.

The wedding of Leah and her betrothed takes place shortly afterwards. However, just as the ceremony is about to conclude, the bride is possessed by a dybbuk—the wandering soul of Chanon, her true love, who was not allowed to enter Paradise for his presumption in forbidden prayer. When Leah arises she has become strange. She dances around the village, dervish-like, propelled by the spirit of the dybbuk. Finally, she is taken to the village of the chief exorcist rabbi. A magic circle is drawn about her and the dybbuk expelled as he cries out that he will never leave her. But "love conquers all," for when Leah awakens from the exorcist's trance, she hears the voice of Chanon calling to her and drawing her out of the circle of supernatural protection. She falls to the ground dead, outside the circle, and the audience hears the voices of the lovers happy to be reunited, now to be wandering spirits forever.

Watching a 1970 version of the play performed in Los Angeles, I was struck by the psychological force of the intensely dramatic piece.

vi / Introduction

The dybbuk seemed to me to be a symbol for the way eros love dominates the entire person—will, heart, spirit, and body. In fantasy, the lover who is outwardly rejected, for whatever reason, believes that he or she cannot live without the beloved and longs to enter the other in a fusion which could never be dissolved. The dybbuk is, however, not only a symbol of the lover, but also the spirit of the lover actually dwelling in the beloved in an immaterial yet palpable manner. Death becomes the only manner of bringing about an end to the remaining physical difference between the two already united souls.

Certainly, in the play, *The Dybbuk*, the overtones are demonic rather than holy. Yet the image haunts, carrying within itself a truth about all romantic love, even with a happy ending, because of the so primordial depiction of love's need for total possession of the all-beautiful beloved.

Is it possible to "baptize" the symbol of the dybbuk in the exploration of union of a spiritual and holy kind? To explain what I have in mind, I will relate an experience and then try to analyze it in more universal terms.

For years, as you will see from the letters, the relationship between Charles Rich and myself was both close and sublime in nature, but still far from a complete union. This was not because of distance of place, but rather came from a disparity between the infused contemplation characterizing the prayer life of Charles, and my own much more sporadic glimpses of the divine. There was much more of me and less of Christ in my spiritual life than in his, and so I couldn't really keep up with him, even though I was inspired by his thoughts.

Then, in 1982, after an act of consecration to the Immaculate Heart of Mary, I was quite suddenly drawn into mystical prayer and also into daily correspondence with Charlie, for he was the only person I knew well whom I could count on to understand my experience.

Very soon I began to find that in the midst of such "bathing" in God's ineffable grace, the very spirit of Charlie would enter my own. Somewhat playfully, I began to call this a "holy dybbuk" encounter. As you will read, Charlie himself loved the play *The Dybbuk*, and thought the expression apt, even if a new coinage.

Now, one of the strongest themes running through the letters of

Introduction / vii

Charles Rich is that of the way spiritual love in Christ is a foretaste of heaven. Already in this life, if we are careful to purify our love of anything not of Him, we can experience the joy of the union of persons which will be ours completely in eternity.

And so, I boldly dub my great friend "the holy dybbuk"—for in his daring prayers of unity with God and with those given to him as gifts of God, he truly knows how to enter into the very fiber of the being of the beloved.

My prayer is that even though you, the reader, may not have known Charles Rich personally, the fire of the love with which the Holy Spirit has infused this writer of such passionate letters may enter your own heart. May you come to know through him, as I have, more of the "height, length, the depths, of the love that is in Christ Jesus."

The Holy Dybbuk
Letters of Charles Rich, Contemplative

June 11, 1960

Dear Ronda,

You shot like a meteor into my life and, for a person who has received the grace to become a Catholic, there can be only one explanation for such a thing. God wants you to become a saint, for that is your real vocation as it is the vocation of everyone who has received the gift of the true faith.

We meet on earth in order that we should have the happiness that comes from being able to be together in heaven, and so you should ask for the grace to be able to think of this every time God puts you in contact with another human being. I shall always pray for you the grace that you should love Him very much and in the way He has said we should, that is, with everything that's in us and which we have from His goodness.

We should love God with our whole heart and with our whole mind, and it's very evident from the few times I have spoken to you that you have been given the grace to do this. Life is short, so there is little opportunity to give ourselves completely up to the pursuit of what we shall know and love forever in the life to come.

Read the psalms and for that matter any other portion of the Sacred Scriptures, and you will soon realize how all that matters is that which is of a nature to last forever. We must build for eternity and make eternity the sole quest of our lives. This may sound a little preachy, but all I am trying to say is that you should reserve all the love of your heart and mind for Him who has, out of His infinite love for you, given you this heart and this mind.

A saint said that we can all become saints because we all have hearts with which to love and bodies with which to suffer. There are infinite ways to loving God with the same passionate ardor with which all the saints loved Him, and so there can be no excuse for your not being ranked one day in their own blessed society.

Become a saint Ronda, or rather ask God to make you one, and all the problems you now have will be solved. You can become a saint, for St. Francis de Sales says that "there are as many different kinds of sanctities as there are saints." And though it is now too early to know

4 / *The Holy Dybbuk*

exactly what place God has for you in His Mystical Body, the one occupied by each saint was meant by Him for every one of them. Does it not state in the Scripture: "Be you holy as your Father in heaven in holy"?

Excuse my preaching, Ronda, I am merely trying to say you should love the Divine Good, Beauty, and Truth God is, with the utmost of your ability, for that is what it means to be a saint. Everyone who believes in the true faith can, if he so wills, receive the grace from God to do this.

God would not ask us to do and be what is beyond our power to achieve, and so when He asks us all to become saints, He realizes that we are able to carry out this divine injunction. We, of course, don't have to love God with the same ardor and intensity with which the saints loved Him in order to save our souls. But if we don't, we miss so much joy in this life, for it's right here and now that the saints receive a taste of the infinite bliss they shall have forever after they leave this life. Become a saint and you will perceive what is unexperienced by those who do not do all they are able to cooperate completely with the grace of God.

This letter is getting out of hand, so I will close with my best regards to you, Carla,* and your dear mother—remember me to both. Your dear friend in all that's of a nature to last forever.

Charlie

*[*Carla is my twin sister. She became a Catholic five years after I did; my mother some ten years afterwards.*—Ed.]

September 4, 1960

Dear Ronda,

. . . I have been rereading the Book of Job this morning and it struck me what a wonderful source of consolation and help it is to us in times of real trouble when the soul is tempted to feel life is too much for anyone to be able to bear. I had read and reread and studied this book for years before my conversion, and it was even then a source of great strength to me. I say before my conversion because I did not then yet have the grace to look upon the Bible as the Inspired Word of God.

Letters of Charles Rich / 5

And if it was even then such a source of help, you can imagine what the reflection upon its words does for my soul now when I believe it to be the exact words of Him by Whom we have been loved so much from all eternity.

If you will allow me, I would like to recommend the reading, studying, and reflection and contemplation of it at this time in your young life when there are so many important problems to be met in the search you make to get to know who and what God is, so that you may in that way get to love all His Holy Name stands for.

It is interesting to reflect on the fact that two of the most learned mystics the Church has produced—St. John of the Cross and St. Gregory the Great—have made this book the mainstay of their lives and have commented so much upon it. St. Gregory the Great has made the devout study of it the main task of his life, for he has written about two thousand pages of commentary on this book alone, and this commentary can still be had in an English translation. . . . If you could read and reread for a long time, you would find no problem that comes up in your life on which it would not throw light.

It was the favorite spiritual reading of St. Thomas Aquinas. St. Teresa of Avila and St. John of the Cross quote profusely from it. I know of no book better able to pull anyone through the dark and difficult stages on his journey to intimate union with Our Divine Lord, since it was written for this purpose. It is *the* commentary on the Book of Job, and so far, nothing equal to its profundity exists, as Gregory states that he was inspired to write it in order to find the help he required to face the difficulties of a life of holiness. If you are in pain or trouble of any kind, this is and should be the book for you. . . .

A saint once said that the sufferings we go through and which are borne by us out of love for God, serve as a "staircase to paradise." This is a very beautiful and helpful thought, but there is one which is even more beautiful and more helpful, and it comes to us from the mouth of St. Thomas of Villanova. St. Thomas has this to say in reference to the sufferings we go through, and the anxiety we have that they should serve us as a means of union with our dearest wishes for what is substantially Divine. "You will find Him not in words but in wounds; not in thoughts, but in anguish," for so far no way has yet been found to

6 / *The Holy Dybbuk*

things Divine but the one trodden by the Son of God and that Way is the Way of the Cross.

Well, Ronda, I am praying that all you now go through by way of suffering should serve to bring you closer to the God you love so much and it certainly will if you want it to. There is one particular passage in the Book of Job which has for many years prior to my conversion been a great source of strength to me in the many troubles of my life and it occurs in the eleventh chapter of that book. Speaking of the trials and troubles of this gravely afflicted saint, his friend "Sophar" has this to say to him—and to us also, if we so will—"you shall forget your misery, or recall it like waters that have ebbed [passed] away." What can be more consoling for you to read in the condition you say in your letter you are now in. I hope and pray that God will give you the grace you will always need to extract the wisdom and beauty and strength the Holy Scriptures contain in them, for if you turn to them, they will heal all your ills like medicine does the ills of the body.

Pray for me as I do for you. Regards to everyone at home,

Charlie

I pray for you that you and everyone you love in this world should find yourself in heaven someday and that you will thank all your friends for the help they give you to get you there—I hope to be included among these friends.

September 30, 1960

Dear Ronda,

...It's easy to cope with the problems of life if we get the grace to realize this world is not our *real* home, but only a sort of makeshift. St. Teresa of Avila has a very good expression in this respect, and she calls it a sort of stage-play. Many years before my conversion, I got the grace to realize this world *is not my true home*, and it was this realization that helped me overcome the problems I had. I think if you will start building another world than this in your soul, you can always take refuge in it from the troubles that will come up. We have to have another world to which to flee as to a city of refuge. There is another life to come and it's this life that counts. Everything else is of no

Letters of Charles Rich / 7

importance because it will not last, for there comes an end to all created good things as well as to what is bad.

Get this truth fixed firmly in your soul, and you will see how quickly it will serve to act in it as a balm from heaven.

We take this life too seriously and that's where all the troubles lie. God did not intend we should think too much about passing goods, and it is our fault if by taking them too seriously we become over-concerned about them. This life is nothing, for compared to the one to come it doesn't even deserve the name of being.

You have a lot of problems because you are still young, but many of them will disappear with your growing years. I would like to help you climb the steep road of holiness, because I know it's only thus you will find any kind of happiness in this life and the peace you are looking for—*shalom*. And I would do anything in the world to help you attain it. You must make sanctity the main aim of your life and everything else subordinate to it, for this alone will succeed in solving all your problems.

Charlie

Pray for me, Ronda, and I assure you I shall always pray for you. Excuse my sermonizing tone.

[*A priest told Charlie never to preach but only to love, and so, from time to time, he apologizes for any such presumed preachiness.*—Ed.]

October 4, 1960

Dear Ronda,

I don't know if I have so far mentioned to you the name of St. Francis de Sales and the enormous influence the reading of his great master-piece, *The Treatise on the Love of God* has had upon my life. If I have not, I will make this book the main object of this letter.

I first came across him accidentally as I was browsing in the public library. I saw this book there and after sampling a few of its pages, it seemed there was nothing of any value in it for me. A little later, I saw my very learned and holy spiritual director, and he asked if I had read the writings of this great Doctor of the Church. I said I did, but did not like them. He told me to try again.

8 / *The Holy Dybbuk*

I did, and for the next fifteen years this book became one of my favorite spiritual and mystical works. I still re-read it now and then and the contents are timeless as far as I am concerned. There is a humanism in it which makes Christian truths acceptable to those who would otherwise feel no attraction for them, and it has won the praise of all the great masters of the spiritual life who have ever written on this theme, namely, the love of God for man and how to successfully attain union with Him.

...I can do nothing better for you than to urge you to make this work one of your main supports and stand-bys. I hope you will find everything here of interest and of help, and pray for the compiler.

Your dear friend,

Charlie

October 6, 1960

Dear Ronda,

In glancing through your letter again, I noticed a question there I did not even begin to answer: you ask, "But how do you find out what God wants you to do?" You find out what God wants you to do by the same process by which you learn anything else you wish to become proficient in and master, namely, by continually trying to accomplish what you set out to do.

You learn how to play a musical instrument by continual practice and everything else in the same way and an element of time and experience enters into all these efforts.

You are still a very, very young girl, so don't expect to achieve now what can only be attained with the passing of the years and which same bring insight and wisdom with them not to be had in the time of our youth. You will have to wait until you get a little older to find the clear answers to many of your problems along spiritual lines, and diligent exercise of your mental powers will help you do so. You will have to read an awful lot of first class spiritual classics, for it is God's will our minds should be enlightened through their means.

"When we read, God speaks to us, and when we pray, we speak to Him." These words have become classical and they are those

Letters of Charles Rich / 9

expressed by all the great doctors of the Church beginning with St. Augustine. Does not St. Paul himself say to us: "Attend unto reading"? What clearer hint on the part of Almighty God is there that it is His will that our knowledge of Him should in this life come to us by means of the books you read.

After you have spent many years reading all the great masterpieces of Christian literature, you will begin to see that many of the questions your mind now asks can only be understood after you have assimilated the profound writings of the doctors of the Church, for God has inspired them to write down all that enters into our heart and mind, for the Holy Bible is only part of His message to us. The rest of it is contained in the works of the great saints of the Church, especially those gifted with the power of communicating to others all God has infused into their own souls.

As to the question of copying persons whom you admire, there is certainly nothing wrong with this save that you take care to admire the right kind of people, those whose lives square with all they say. I think it was Millet who spent many years in the Louvre doing nothing else but copying the great masterpieces that he admired in that place. It was only after long arduous practice of this kind that he had the courage to do his own painting.

Did you ever come across a great master in painting or sculpture who did not have a model from which to create his masterpiece? Our models are the saints, for that's the reason God brings them into this world, and have not all the saints copied from one another? Did not St. Ignatius Loyola say: "What St. Francis did, I can do"? All the saints had someone to teach them the science of holiness and it was usually another saint like themselves. The saints learned from one another what God wanted them to do and that's why it's so important to read their lives.

The great masters of the spiritual life all insist that next to the study of the Holy Scriptures we have to master all that the saints have written down throughout the last nineteen hundred years, for it's only in this way we will become intimately acquainted with what is God's will in our regard. You have a lot of work ahead of you in this respect, but it's going to pay off very well to you in the long run. There is not a

10 / *The Holy Dybbuk*

problem a human being ever had which was not successfully faced by some saint. You have a lot of problems which may now baffle you. If you keep on reading the lives of the saints, you will find that nothing has ever come up in your own spiritual life which has not already occurred in the life of some saint.

... Keep on fighting the good fight St. Paul speaks about and which consists in always striving for the heights along spiritual and intellectual lines. Become a giant in the spiritual life and you will find the altitude bracing and refreshing to your soul. Don't be satisfied with anything but the best along this line. Fight, and the Lord of battles— spiritual ones—will come to your assistance. He loves brave and daring hearts.

Charlie

November 9, 1960

Dear Ronda,

I have to warn you that in your relationship with me and, for that matter, that with any other human being whatsoever, you have to be careful not to be too dependent upon him, but upon Him by whom that human being has been made, since it is an axiom of the Church that whatever good is in anyone, that good comes to him from God and not from himself.

It's true God wants us to have deep intimate associations with each other, for that is the basis of the doctrine of the Mystical Body of Christ, and yet, by the same token, it is also equally important for us to realize that whatever we get from others as the result of this relationship comes to us from God and that these same people whom we rightfully love and cherish are only the channels which, for a reason we shall never know on this earth, God is pleased to make use of but on which He, being what He is, can in no way depend.

It is consoling for us to think of this, because it makes us realize that God is everywhere and so we can always have from Him whatever we stand in need of either for the well-being of our body or our soul.

It's okay to look forward to seeing those we love and cherish in Christ, but it's equally important to consider that God Himself can always give us what we derive through their means and St. Paul refers

Letters of Charles Rich / 11

to this as to a kind of liberty of spirit, for while it's all right to derive help from others, it is equally important to know that God has no need of anyone in order to endow our souls with what they need for their salvation and sanctification.

Did not some of the most gigantic individuals acquire sanctity with no one around to help them, like St. Anthony of the Desert and others like him?

God is always around, Ronda, and all you have to do is to humbly call upon Him for help in all your troubles and He will be more than willing to be of assistance to you in whatever trials and difficulties that can come up in your spiritual life.

If you drop into some church, you will be face to face with Him Who IS Wisdom in Essence and Nature, and He will answer any question you can put to Him and provide you with all you need to become a saint. By the way, don't worry about the temptation that you have no right to want to become as holy as a human being is able to become in this life, for all the saints who have ever lived had to go through the same temptation, for though the devil won't mind you becoming just another good Catholic, he will rant and rave when he sees you entertaining hopes to become a saint instead.

The devil hates everything that's first class and so he is always ready to put up a big fuss when he sees anyone harboring ideas which all the saints have had, those namely of walking side by side with Him Who once walked this earth, and if there is one thing he will always hate it will be the thought of people like yourself becoming a saint as great as anyone the Church has produced.

The devil hates greatness in spirituality and he loves mediocrity in it. That is why he puts so many obstacles in the way of greatness in that field. . . .

The devil. . . will do all in his power to suggest that you are guilty of tempting God by your presumption. When he does so, don't pay any attention and he will soon stop bothering you along that line. He is a very proud spirit and so he can't stand being humiliated by defeats. "Resist the devil," we are told in the Scriptures, "and he will depart from you."

We have to put up an effort to get rid of the moods that come over us

12 / The Holy Dybbuk

and which same are a source of depression to the soul, and if more people fought a little more valiantly along that line, there would be less work for psychiatrists, for the reason they are kept so busy is because people give in too easily and they don't go out of their way to make greater efforts to overcome their evil inclinations to be depressed.

God hates sad souls and He goes on to tell us so in many parts of the Scriptures. I could quote endlessly along that line but I won't have enough time to do it in.

You should never take your depressed moods too seriously and especially those relating to your inability to be more perfect than you are, for such moods have their origin in him, who even if he wished, could not know the joy there will always be in truly confiding hearts— don't you remember what it says in the psalms of such people? Do they not tell us more than once that such a person is like a tree planted near running water, that yields its fruit in due season and whose leaves never fade? And what do these same psalms tell us of those who are opposite to them? Do they not say, "Not so the wicked, not so; they are like chaff which the wind drives away."

There should be nothing but holy joy in your heart and if it's not there you ought to make it your business that it should be there as soon as possible, for a person like you with all the gifts with which you have been blessed by an infinitely good God, should have everything to make you full of gratitude and keep thanking Him all the time. "I will bless the Lord all the time," the Hebrew text states.

If the Psalmist could have occasion to make this statement, you should be able to do the same thing, since the hand of God has not been shortened, for what He has done for those in the past, He is more than ready to do for people like yourself.

It's He who has made great saints of the men and women who have lived in times gone by, and so it's your own fault if you fail to rise as high in holiness as any other human being who has ever lived has attained—and don't be afraid of presumption in this regard, for that is a temptation planted in you by the father of lies and you know who he is: Satan in all his subtle disguises.

I am writing all this to encourage you to hope that you will become a

Letters of Charles Rich / *13*

great saint someday, for it is in the attainment of high holiness that happiness in this life can be obtained, for the holier you will become, the more joyful your interior being will be and you will live until the day when you will be compelled to say how true this is.

Too many people are unhappy and it's due to their lack of holiness, since holiness is the health of the soul and the lack of it, its infirmity. It's not a luxury to become a saint, it is a dire necessity, since without it, life on this earth would become unendurable—it would be so for me personally, for I can't see how I could go on living another minute without the hope of holiness rooted deeply within myself.

There was a time when sanctity was not my ideal and that was a time when I was nearest to the state in which they are who will never for all eternity be able to love what is true, beautiful, and good. I feel sorry for people who do not nurture themselves on the thoughts the saints kept uppermost in their minds, for I cannot see how they have the strength to go on meeting the many trials and difficulties that come up in this life.

So take a cue from those who have succeeded in mastering the art of living, the saints, and with them "rejoice in the Lord, again I say, rejoice," as St. Paul says to everyone he knows and whom he wishes to see as happy as it is possible for anyone to be in this world.

If you make sanctity the only ideal of your life, the problems you now have will one day be solved—that I can guarantee you from my own personal experience. For though I have nothing but God, He is sufficient for all my needs, for in having Him, what is it we cannot have with Him? Is He not the sole source of every good, true, and beautiful thing, and do we not have this in substance when we have Him, the Substantial Good? We not only have this Good, but we are in some marvelous way so immingled with It that we are "oned" in that Good, so that He is what we are and we are what He is, for that is the meaning of the text from the Song, "I belong to him and he belongs to me." And does not St. Paul confirm this when he says that we are made the partakers of the Divine Nature?

. . . You're now in the position of someone going through the territory in which he has never set foot, and so it's natural for you to be afraid. But as your knowledge of the mystical ways of God increases,

14 / *The Holy Dybbuk*

you will get less concerned and will walk the paths of sanctity with a greater degree of firmness.

It's one thing to go through a dark tunnel and not know from personal experience that the light will soon appear and quite another to have gone through that same tunnel over and over again, and so the darkness no longer becomes an object of apprehension. I have been through a whole lot of dark spiritual tunnels and the blackness of them has often been a source of alarm to me. The time will come when you, too, will be in the same position, and so you will then be able to be of comfort to others who have not yet traveled that way. You are only a young girl yet and so there are vast areas in the ways of God you have not yet gone through.

When you grow older spiritually, the troubles you now have will completely disappear and you will then thank God for the experiences that have enriched your knowledge and love of Him.

You are on the right path, and so the thing for you is to ask God for the grace to stay on it, and this, according to the greatest theologians the Church has produced, is no small favor, for it is nothing to have been given the grace to begin if we are through our own fault deprived of the grace to finish what we have begun, for it is only they who persevere to the end that Our Lord says shall be saved. With this thought I bid you farewell.

Charlie

November 11, 1960

Dear Ronda,

. . . I would like to say something this morning which ought to be of great help in meeting the problems that will come in your future life in the Church and in the effort you will make to attain close union with Our Divine Lord, and it consists in your being able to take things as they come, the good as well as the bad, consolations as well as desolations. In the spiritual life nothing remains the same from one day to the next, and it all is subject to the laws of variation and change, for just as it is sometimes sunny and other times not so in the physical order, so in the same way is it sometimes good weather in the soul and other times bad weather. But the experienced person in the things of God should make it his or her business to make use of whatever happens in order to bring him or her closer to the goal on which he or she has been set by God, so that if we feel low or high we should nevertheless strive to remain essentially the same as far as the superior portion in ourselves is concerned. . . .

As you know so well by now, from the spiritual authors you have thus far read, the life of the soul in its relationship with things Divine has often been compared with the state of two people who first fall in love with each other and then consummate that love by means of marriage.

At first there is the beautiful romance of getting to know each other, then the intimacy, then the wedding day, and after the wedding day comes the prosaic problems of having children, taking care of them, cooking the meals and keeping the house, which entails quite a lot of hum-drum and monotony, so much so, that after the honeymoon stage, a lot of these couples get bored with each other's company and the task of raising a family becomes so wearisome that they separate and that's the end to that wonderful career which started out with such high promise of happiness to come.

Milton refers to this happiness between such two people in the words of *Paradise Lost* which read "emparadised in each other's arms," or something very similar. I read this poem too long ago to remember the exact words.

Well this "Paradise" in the form of love between two people often ends up on the rocks because these people wanted the sun to shine on them all the time, and so when bad weather came into their relationship with each other, they lost heart and quit because they were too weak and soft to live up to the responsibilities of their state.

The same is true when God espouses our souls, because, when He first does so, He gives us a lot of graces which for our own good He mercifully later on withholds from us, and unless we are trained and exercise ourselves in the school of the Cross, we get like a lot of weak and half-hearted people who wanted sugar and candy all the time and not the plain bread the soul has to eat in order to flourish and grow strong.

I know a highly educated and cultured Jewish convert girl who, after

16 / The Holy Dybbuk

living a deeply spiritual life for ten years, receiving Holy Communion each day and reading mystical and ascetical authors, threw the whole thing away and left the Church. The reason she gives is that she never really believed in any of these things but did them out of routine. However, I happen to know that the cause is quite different, for she was unable to find someone to go out with and so picked out a married man and now lives with him.

The remarkable thing about this girl is that she was deeply spiritual and would talk of nothing else but prayer and contemplation, the liturgy, and so on. Her whole soul seemed to be dead-centered on the things of the spirit and yet after an intense life like this she walks off and leaves the whole thing as if she had never known what God and consolations of Faith, Hope, and Love were like.

What happened to this highly gifted Jewish convert girl who could not do enough in her effort to unite her soul with Our Lord? Fundamentally, it will always remain a mystery, but partially it may be explained by the fact that she refused to make the sacrifices inherent in being a spouse of Christ; she wanted to have the cake and eat it at the same time. For in the spiritual life as well as in the life of any worthwhile occupation, there are sacrifices to be borne, and unless we make up our minds that we must take the good with the bad, the pleasant with the unpleasant, the trials as well as the consolations, we will never succeed in persevering in the goal which we have set out to attain. The spiritual life has its crosses; it has its keen disappointments, its trials and bitterness of every conceivable variety, and unless we prepare ourselves ahead of time in order to bear them well, we will not succeed in doing so when they will inevitably come to us.

There will be days on which you will get depressed even as all the saints have been depressed, but like the saints you will have to do all that's in your power to fight it off and not give into it as to some sweet and perverted luxury.

Was not Job depressed? Was not Moses so when he asked God to take him out of this world because he could not stand the sight of human depravity? Were not all the prophets of the Old Testament depressed? For otherwise why did Jeremiah say: "Cursed be the day in which I was born." But the difference between them and others

Letters of Charles Rich / 17

consists in their refusal to give in to this depression and in their turning to God in order to get the grace to fight it off.

You have been given the grace to be a Catholic and you have the remedies for whatever ills can come up in your life and it's your duty to make proper use of them. Of course, the devil will tempt you as he has done all the saints and make you feel miserable and disgusted with both your own self and everything around you. But that's the test of a strong soul, for weak ones give in and listen to the suggestions he makes; like Judas of old they take his advice and go out and hang themselves.

The devil hates you because he hates God, and not being able to inflict any harm on Him, he gets his revenge by trying to injure those whom God loves. Not being able to beat up the father of a child because of the superiority of his strength, he beats up the helpless and defenseless child of that father.

There will come dry and monotonous days in your spiritual life, for God will try to find out if you love Him or the gifts He gives you. He did the same thing to all his saints, like Job, but what did Job do when everything God gave him was allowed to be taken away from him by the power of the devil? Did he obey his unbelieving wife who told him to "curse God and die"? The answer he gave was, "We accept good things from God, and should we not accept evil?" This is the answer you have to make to your own soul when things don't turn out the way you, in your finite mind, think they should.

I could give you another case of a gifted Jewish convert who left the Church because he did not pray for the grace to make the sacrifice entailed in being a Catholic. Everyday both those who are born into the Faith and those who come to it from the outside quit the Church because they are unwilling to put up with the drab monotony there often is in living a spiritual life: they know nothing of the terrible trials the saints had to go through in order to remain faithful to the end, and so they throw in the sponge and are unhappy for the remainder of their earthly days, to say nothing of the eternity of joys they could have had if they had a little more spunk in them to fight the good fight everyone has to wage in order to fulfill the duties of his state.

I could quote you a whole book which deals with the trials and

18 / *The Holy Dybbuk*

temptations the saints had to go through every day of their earthly lives in order to convince you that, spiritually speaking, there are four seasons in the life of those who give themselves to God, and so we can't expect it to be spring and summer all the time.

In heaven alone we will be able to repeat the words of the *Song*: "For see, the winter is past, the rains are over and gone" (2:11). By winter is here meant the many trials and afflictions of this life which shall never fully cease till we are no longer in this life, for as long as we shall live, it shall be true of us as it was of all the saints, for "the saints spent the greater part of their lives in affliction and darkness"—these words are from St. Alphonsus Ligouri and so they cannot be questioned.

Many saints were tempted to commit suicide, and this years after they had had the most sublime visions of God any human being is able to experience in this life, because that's the way we have to work out our sanctification in this life. For the more we are loved, the greater will be the trials we will be allowed to have as proof of this love. We are free not to bear them in a Christlike way, and that's why so many who suffer do not become the saints they could have been had they borne their sufferings in the right way.

This is getting to be quite a long letter, but it won't do you any real harm to read it, for all I say in it has already been repeated over and over again by all the saints who have ever lived. What is it they keep on reiterating over and over again but the truth that suffering is the key of heaven and it's the greatest grace a human being can have in this life. For happiness, according to the saints and all the great masters of the spiritual life, does not consist in having sublime visions of God and personal experience of His Infinite Goodness and Beauty. The saints had all this and yet found it did not make them the happy human beings they felt they were meant by God to be.

Happiness consists in bearing the trials and troubles of this life exactly in the same way as Our Lord bore them when He was on this earth, and as they were borne by those who went ahead of Him, the Patriarchs and Prophets of the Old Testament.

Happiness consists in doing what Moses and David did when they went through the trials and afflictions of their earthly lot, and if you want to know what this is, read the words spoken by them; read the

Letters of Charles Rich / 19

psalms, for in them you will find the sweet singer of Israel telling you how he bore his own troubles and how you should bear yours.

Saul, on the other hand, did not pray for the grace to do the same thing, and so he gave into the devil's suggestion that he should end his own life. The saints stood their ground and fought manfully whenever any dark and depressing thought occurred to them; they refused to give into the temptation to be bored and weary of life, and that's why they now reign in the glory of their heavenly bliss.

You *can* do the same thing and you *have* to do the same thing, for unless you do, you won't have the grace to remain on the road on which God set you when He made you a Catholic, for it's one grace to turn to God and be converted to Him, but quite another to persevere on to the last breath of your life. Unless we fight we shall not be crowned since "no cross, no crown" is the motto of the Church.

In the spiritual life you have to sometimes eat plain bread without any butter on it, and sometimes cake. The days on which you have to eat plain bread are more numerous than the others, for the bread, in the form of trials, has more nourishment in it than the cake of consolations, so God lets us have the former as well as the latter.

Goodby for awhile, and I'll write again sometime.

Charlie

March 24, 1961

Dear Ronda,

I prayed for you this morning at Mass and asked God to make you a saint. I hope you are not afraid of my use of this word in reference to you, because many Catholics are. They don't know its true meaning and fear the sacrifices God would ask of them in order that they may be made His dear and intimate friends. I ask God to make you a saint and I hope that you ask Him to make one of me also. For unless we become saints our purpose in life has been in vain. Do you recall the words of a recent French Catholic writer—he said that the only tragedy in life is not to have been a saint.

I agree wholeheartedly with him and my only interest in you lies in the fact that I am convinced it's God's holy will you should, by the way you live, join the ranks of the great women the Church has produced

20 / *The Holy Dybbuk*

like St. Catherine of Siena, St. Gertrude the Great, St. Teresa of Avila and all others like them.

I am asking great things from God in your behalf and I want you to join me in your prayers for them. God is infinitely powerful and so why cannot He make a saint of a person like you? He can and He will, if only you want to become one. Want to become one, for it is in your power to have such a desire. In this regard, be a woman of desires and God will do for you what He did for others who wanted to have Him very much.

The angel Gabriel appeared to Daniel because he found him to be a man of desires. "From the beginning of thy prayers," he says to him, "the word came forth, and I am now come to show it to thee, because thou art a man of desires" (Daniel 9:23). What can be clearer than this that God wants each one of us to have great and holy desires so that we may in this way become worthy and capable of receiving from Him all He wishes to give us.

Become a saint and all your problems will soon be solved; they will be solved by the graces you will receive and which will act as a light to your soul and strength to fulfill all God expects from you as the result of His having created you in His own image and likeness.

As I read your letters, I am heartened with joy at the thought that you love Christ so much. You must realize that you do so with His own love, the love He Himself has placed into your heart for Himself.

Never mind your vices and shortcomings which will be with you as long as you remain in the body of this death, its flesh weakened and vitiated by sin and so you will always have something to keep you humble and dependent upon God's grace, for that alone is sufficient for all your needs.

We don't have to be perfect in this life but only have the desire and will to be so; we will attain perfection as soon as the soul will leave the body to which it is at present so mysteriously united. Then you will be and do that which you had all your life wanted to.

Till then, though, you will have to have the charity, patience, and deep humility to be able to put up with yourself and expect no miracles in that direction, for all the saints whom the Church has canonized have had to do the same thing and had the same problems that you, and everyone else who loves God in this life, have. They all asked God that He should remove the "thorn from their flesh" of which St. Paul speaks in the twelfth chapter of the Second Epistle to the Corinthians. But what was the answer he received? He was told that for his own good that thorn has to remain with him 'til the time comes for him to die, for it's only then we can safely be without something to cause us deep humiliation. For in this life, with all the dangers there are to our pride, we need some weakness, some failing in our make-up to keep us humble. Otherwise the good things we receive from God could cause us to think we are superior in virtue to those around us.

You will always be confronted with some sort of humiliating misery in yourself, but it will be there for a very good purpose.

...As God says to St. Paul, "My grace is sufficient for thee, for strength is made perfect in weakness." How is strength made perfect in weakness? Pray, and God will enlighten your mind to understand how this is possible....

As regards the doctrine of the Mystical Body of Christ, I have read quite a few books on this subject but so far they have not made it any clearer to me. St. Thomas Aquinas refers to this doctrine somewhere in the *Summa* and alongside with it he mentions the fact that there is also a Mystical Body of Satan as well. I think if you are particularly observant in the affairs of men, it becomes quite clear that there are these two mystical bodies at work in the world, for they are both powerfully organized and they are both engaged in an unrelenting warfare with one another. Is not the Mystical Body of Satan clearly at work in the Communist countries of the world, and is not that Body of his engaged in bitter conflict with the Mystical Body of Christ?

There is a Mystical Body all right, and we can perceive its existence both among those who are good and those whose lives are evil. The Psalmist talks about these two bodies when he says "Happy the man who follows not the counsel of the wicked, nor walks in the way of sinners, nor sits in the company of the insolent, but delights in the law of the Lord and meditates on his law day and night." Here we have these two contrasts of those whose lives are good and those whose lives are evil and they exist side by side, for just as Christ is the Head of those who are good, so Satan is of those who are bad.

If you read the New Testament, you will find this doctrine even

22 / *The Holy Dybbuk*

more explicitly stated, for Satan is there referred to as the "prince of this world" (John 13:31).

I don't know if these few words on this subject will afford you any satisfaction, but if you think of Christ with faith and hope and love and let yourself become completely absorbed in His infinite goodness and beauty, you will soon become intimately acquainted with all that is necessary for your personal sanctification, for to know and love Him is to have all your problems solved. Christ will always be the only solution to all the problems a human being can have in this life, so why not turn to Him for such a purpose?

Become completely absorbed in Christ, as a sponge in water, so that His Being will penetrate your being and of the two there will be made one. "Christ before me, Christ behind me," so run the words supposed to have been uttered by St. Patrick. Let Christ completely dominate your life so that there will be no room in it for anything else but Him, and you will soon see in a mystical way how everything the Church teaches is true. You will come to know this by your personal experience of Him by Whom you have been redeemed, for I myself have always found this experience to be the solution for all my problems.

Stay close to Our Divine Lord and make His thoughts and His sentiments your own. Permit yourself to become so completely impregnated with what is of a nature to last forever that what Christ is you will be. . . .

Prayer is the deepest and most intimate contact one soul can have with another, and that is the kind of relationship I ask God should always exist between us. I shall always pray for you because it's in that way I can express myself best in your regard. May God make of you what He has already done for so many of His holy and chosen souls, and may you, by His mercy and love, be joined in their own blessed ranks.

Goodby in Him,

Charlie

P.S.   I have just passed my twenty-eighth birthday as a Catholic. I was very ill when I entered the Church and sincerely hoped I could go to heaven as soon as possible. God saw otherwise, so here I am still so very far away from Home. I'll pray for you when I get there.

Letters of Charles Rich / 23

April 2, 1961

Dear Ronda,

You are reaching a point in your relationship with God where only a priest is able to give you advice and answer the questions you ask in your last letter; for though a layman like myself or anyone else has both the knowledge and the other qualities by which this can be done, the answer he will give you will lack the necessary authority and you will receive no grace therefrom. [*This letter began a long battle on this point, as I was receiving direction from a very holy layperson—not Charlie—and he thought I should see a priest, preferably a Jesuit. I am presently under the direction of a holy Jesuit priest, but still believe that a layperson can be a fine director.*—Ed.]

You will have to put yourself into the hands of a priest and follow his advice like a child does that of his mother or a pupil that of his teacher in class. We cannot find out what God wants us to do in this life, or the particular state we should embrace, in any other way. "Go to the priest," God says to those who want to know what He does or does not want as far as they are concerned, and though the priest they go to may be inferior to them by way of learning, and even holiness of life, it is still the will of God that to him we should go and that there should be no substitute.

Laymen are all right to encourage us to become holy and grow in the love and knowledge of God, but they lack the power to lead us to him. We are led to him by the authority of those whom God has ordained for that purpose, for what is a priest but another Christ, and what is the purpose of Christ but to lead us to His Father in heaven? You will have to go to some priest and ask him the questions you do in your last letter, for he alone has the authority to give you the answer to them that will fill your soul with peace.

I think a lot of your troubles stem from the fact that you fail to realize clearly that it's only at the hands of some priest you can develop yourself in a deeply spiritual way and that a layman is powerless along that line.

You may think by what I say that I am trying to discourage the relationship you have with me, but I can assure you I am not. I know you are sincerely trying to get somewhere from a spiritual point of

24 / The Holy Dybbuk

view, but I also know that there are unalterable laws, laid down by God Himself, concerning the way we should get to Him, and the answers to our questions we should seek along that line.

It is to the priest we have to go to really develop ourselves in a deeply interior way, and anyone I meet who wants to grow in the love and knowledge of God I send to a priest. And though it will always remain true that competent guides along that line will always be difficult to find, this does not absolve us from realizing that there is no one to take the place of God's anointed in that direction. So, with this in view, start praying really earnestly that God should direct you to some competent priest for you to receive the many answers you ask me in your letters. I can give them to you, but you will not receive the graces that come with such answers unless they are given by the proper authorities. . . .

As I said so often, when we like someone in a genuine way, we wish that person well. And what is it we can wish such a person save that which will constitute a source of happiness for him for all eternity—to wish anyone well and to love him in Christ, we ask God that he should become a saint, for nothing less will satisfy the craving in us to see that person happy both in this life and in the next. . .

There is a passage in one of the psalms in which a human being is referred to as a "mere breath of air." That's all we are, Ronda, and so you see from this how utterly useless it is to make too much of either our own selves or anything else in this life, for we are all a kind of divine ray of beauty from the Reality that God alone can be. . .

Pray a lot that God should do for you what He has done for others, for it's through prayer alone we can reach heights of greatness in His eyes.

I don't know what else to say to you, so I bid you farewell in Christ and pray He should truly love you and make you His own blessed one.

Charlie

May 17, 1961

Hello Ronda!

I am sorry that what I said in my last letter caused you pain, for that is the last thing I want to do—not only to you but to any other human

Letters of Charles Rich / 25

being; there is enough suffering in the world for us to want to add to its store of misery and affliction.

I will say, though, that if you want some facts in reference to the matter [*of spiritual direction from a priest vs. a layperson*—Ed.], it would be pertinent to remind you that it was not to a layman St. Teresa of Avila went for direction but to a Jesuit and a Dominican priest. She says herself, in her *Autobiography*, that she was unable to get anywhere in her relationship with God until she spoke to these two Fathers, and it's only after following their advice that she began to make real progress in her prayer life. You can read what she says in her own words.

Then you also have the case of St. Catherine of Siena, perhaps the greatest woman Italy has so far produced, who had Blessed Raymond of Capua for her director. Then you have the case of St. Jane Chantal, who had her St. Francis de Sales, and St. Catherine of Genoa who waited twenty-five years before she was able to find a priest to whom she could go for advice. . . .

But enough of this subject. We will let it go for awhile and pray that God should, in His own good time, guide you to the person who by his skill and advice will enable you to join in the ranks of those I have just mentioned. I want great things for you, Ronda, that's why I talk the way I do, and when you get to heaven, you will there thank me for all eternity that I said what I did to you ever since the first day we met.

. . . What a wonderful thing it is to be able to believe that God became a human being, for we would not otherwise have been able to get so close to Him.

God lives in you, Ronda, as well as in every other human being that exists, so there is no excuse for our not knowing Him. "Do you not know that Jesus Christ is in you?" St. Paul said to those of his own time, and he keeps on saying this to us as well. God is in you and He dwells in the substance of your soul and so we can there touch, taste, and feel Him in a mystical way.

. . . The saints did nothing else in this life but wonder at the beauty and marvelousness of their own being. The realization that they actually existed sent them into rapturous and ecstatic thoughts.

We should be joyfully and holily amazed at our own selves and thank

26 / The Holy Dybbuk

God for having made us out of nothing; we should be amazed at our own body as well as at our soul, since they are both destined to share in God's own Divine Joy for all eternity.

...As long as I will live, I shall continue to ask God to make you completely His, both body and soul, for it's only in this way I can express what God Himself has put into my heart to feel for you.

Do you realize that I am past sixty and so my detention in this existence can't last too long now. When I get to heaven, I shall continue to pray that you, too, should soon get there and that will be the end of all your earthly woes—then only, for as long as you will be on this earth, you will have something to suffer.

..."Ineffable joy in faith alone can move the ungodly, alone too can move the godly to greater godliness. Gaiety, thou art faith in Christ's promise, thou art fruitful in happiness and peace." These words have been spoken by one who has only a few years back been beatified by the Church and who was an authority on Roman law. It's these words of Contardo Ferrini I want to see always in your own soul, for they will bring with them the things they already enjoy who are already in heaven. Goodbye in Our Lord,

Your very dear friend in Him,
Charlie

May 18, 1961

Dear Ronda,

...St. Paul writes: "For I do not understand what I do, for it is not what I wish that I do, but what I hate, that I do. But if I do what I do not wish, I admit that the law is good. Now therefore it is no longer I who do it, but the sin that dwells in me" (Romans 7:16).

It's interesting to note that in Goethe's *Faust* we find a reference to this struggle between the higher and lower part of our nature, for there we read these words: *"Zwei Seelen whonen, ach! in meiner Brust."* [Two souls, alas! reside within my breast." (*Faust*, Pt. I, scene 2)]

It's quite fascinating to see the words of Scripture confirmed by a poet like Goethe, for it strengthens our faith in things divine. I don't know just how much this passage is going to mean to you, but if you

Letters of Charles Rich / 27

reflect on its contents you will find the mystery of your make-up of body and soul a little bit more clear to understand, for at times it seems to us that we are made up of two different and contrary elements, the one that drags us down to base and ignoble things, and the other, which lifts our souls up to the contemplation of things divine.

You will have to go through a lot of hard battles in this life, and they will consist in the warfare against yourself of which both Job and St. Paul have spoken. In Job we read that this whole life of ours is nothing but an unrelenting warfare with ourselves and the forces of evil that drag us to what is infinitely beneath ourselves and which by God's grace we can alone overcome.

It's going to be a long hard struggle, so you will have to arm your soul with the truths of faith and the confirmation of these truths in the great literary masterpieces of the world, like Goethe's *Faust*. I had been reading this great masterpiece before my baptism and found it helpful to bouy up my then drooping and depressing spirit.

I have just now been kind of re-reading it and found it worthy of admiration, even though it has quite a few passages which no Catholic would have dared to write, but, in spite of his sensuous and pagan spirit, *Faust* ends up with the theme of heaven ringing in our ears. . .

Charlie

May 31, 1961

Dear Ronda,

. . .I would like to see the drawing you made of Christ* so send it along the next time you write. If you don't want to part with it, make another one for me because I have a great devotion to well-executed

---

*[*For about six months I tried my hand at artwork. This line drawing had a delightful history: I was too modest to send it to Charlie but gave it years afterwards to a student. She in turn gave it to the Missionaries of Charity in Los Angeles. One day I happened to visit the Missionaries, and there was my old line drawing hanging on the wall. It had found its home.*—Ed.]

28 / *The Holy Dybbuk*

pictures of Our Lord. St. Teresa of Avila said that she felt very sorry for people who have no devotion to pictures of Christ, because they in that way deprive themselves of the help which such pictures would give them. She refers especially to the Protestants of her own day, and she grieved at the harm done by obliterating from our eyes the sight of Him Who had done so much to make us happy, both in time and eternity.

Some saints had extraordinary devotion to holy images and they went out of their way to acquire beautiful executions of them. St. Charles Borromeo had a whole roomful of them, and so we should in no way hesitate to avail ourselves of the help to our soul the loving looking at them would give us.

The Devil always tells people to have a false sense of modesty, a false sense of detachment, a false sense of asceticism, so don't pay any attention when he suggests that you should do without something that will help to love Our Lord better and keep the thought of Him vividly and graphically in your heart.

Get all the holy pictures you can, but see to it they are beautifully executed for God hates bad art. Remember the passage in the Old Testament wherein instructions are given for the building of the first temple? If you read it carefully, you will see that He told Moses to select a very talented and skilled artist by the name of "Beseleel" and had all the beautiful things carved and fashioned by his artistic genius. It's too bad we have such bad art in the Church—but that's enough on this subject.

. . . I will tell you, though, not to let up loving Christ and that you should do so day and night, for He it is on whom the Psalmist meditated "day and night" for He is the "Torah" in which he finds his whole "delight." It's of Him the whole Psalter speaks, for St. Augustine says that he "heard His voice in all the psalms." Learn how to love Him in every single word both of the Old and New Testament since both of these books speak of Him and Him only. "The words of Moses are the words of Christ," St. Jerome tells us, and you can believe what he says because he knew the Bible better than any other human being that ever lived.

. . . Christ died for [all souls] and so what an infinity of beauty,

Letters of Charles Rich / 29

goodness, and truth you and every other soul must be. Love yourself in a holy way, for that's the only way you'll be able to love the creator of that self.

We have to fall in love with that part of ourselves which has been redeemed by the Blood of Christ, for, unless you love your own self, how are you going to love the Maker of that self or any other thing created by Him?

I could talk and talk and talk, but I won't begin to succeed in saying what I would like to tell you along this line, so go into the chapel and ask God to put into your heart what I will ask Him to. It's a relationship in His own Divine love, and so it's in Him and in Him alone I can make myself understood by you—my aim is to get you into heaven, for it's only there I can communicate what I would like to say.

...so keep on striving, for it's in striving for what's sublime that Goethe says we are redeemed. I am quoting this poet because revealed truth is reinforced when it's supported by the natural insights of the great poets of the world, for the natural is a sister to the supernatural and they both have one origin. Did not Our Lord refer to the lilies of the field and does not the word "mountain" occur so frequently in the Scriptures, indicating that God loves everything He has made and that there is nothing in the universe without value in His eyes? He loves what is natural as well as the supernatural. ...

May He always be completely yours, that is my heartiest wish, and I hope you will return the favor by asking God to guide me safely to Himself when my few remaining days are over. If I were a priest, I'd say God bless and keep you forever and ever. I can do this as a layman, but without that special strength given only to God's anointed.

Anyway, this is my sincere wish and always will be for you and all those who are part of you physically and spiritually.

Goodbye in Christ,

Charlie

June 9, 1961

Dear Ronda,

...In reading St. Bernard on the "Song of Songs," you will have to

30 / The Holy Dybbuk

remember that they deal with the most difficult and sublime subject to be found in all the Sacred Writings and that for centuries it had been the custom of the Jewish people not to allow anyone to read the Song of Songs till he or she was over thirty years of age, and this is due to the delicacy of the subject matter.

St. Bernard speaks of three stages of the spiritual life, such as the kiss of the feet, the kiss of the hands, and the kiss of the mouth—this last being bestowed by God only on the soul that has become transformed into Himself by means of His special graces.

The kiss of the feet he says, refers to the first stage in the soul's relationship with things divine, and it is commonly known as the purgative way, in which we do penance for our sins. The kiss of the hands is the practice of all the Christian virtues and is known as the illuminative way. The kiss of the mouth signifies the last stage of the spiritual life in which the soul and God become one by means of transforming union or mystical marriage.

You are still too young for this last stage of the spiritual life, so don't be surprised if you find many things in a writer like Bernard difficult to figure out, for it takes years of experience and hard work to get to know God in an intimate and personal way. However, keep on reading whatever you can in reference to the spiritual life, for if you are diligent and earnest in it, you are bound to get a great deal from anything you read along this line.

As I may have mentioned to you before, I have been reading St. Bernard's commentary on the Song of Songs for about 35 years, and everytime I look through these two volumes of it, I find myself additionally enriched, for to me they are food and nourishment to the soul. We have to eat and drink spiritually as well as take bodily food, and so there is none which affords greater consolation to the soul than these wonderfully sweet and sublime studies or meditations on the Song of Songs.

. . . . We have to have faith in Christ, but it must be a living faith, acted upon and not something we hold in an abstract and theoretical way, for there are plenty of people who believe in God but very few who base their everyday actions on the fact that He is always around and sees every little detail of our earthly existence. Thoreau said that

Letters of Charles Rich / 31

people "make desperate efforts not to live by faith"—so don't become guilty of such an accusation.

It's hard to live by pure faith, and so many people mix it up with that which is contrary to it. It's faith alone that will ultimately solve all our problems, for it's the only way we have of proving we love God in this life. In the life to come we won't need the merit believing in Christ brings with it, for we shall then see Him face to face.

On earth, though, it's the only really worthwhile satisfaction a human being can have, and though as St. Ambrose says, "faith means battles," there is an exhilaration about the war we daily—nay hourly—wage both with our own selves and with everything with which we are surrounded.

I myself have been fighting the good fight St. Paul speaks about for over a period of many years, and this battle did not begin with my entry into the Church but was fought long before that time. I don't think it will surprise you to hear me say that before my conversion I was tempted to take my own life because I found this world too much to bear. But God has always come to my aid, and I am sure He will continue to do so till I won't have to struggle anymore, and this will be the day on which I shall have the blessing to see Him even as I am seen, clearly and openly without the present veil which mortality is.

It's a long hard struggle, Ronda, so don't lose heart no matter what takes place, but think of eternity and that glorious endlessness that will one day be ours in the life to come when there shall be nothing to weep over anymore, and, as the Little Flower so beautifully put it, where there will no longer be "any tombs," for earth is a place of death and heaven the only true life worthy of the name.

"This is the land of death," St. Augustine shrewdly and wisely reminds us, and every day after Mass we recite a prayer in which we refer to our present existence as a "vale of tears." These expressions are not mere euphemisms but the real stark truth, for there is no one on this earth who is completely at peace with himself or completely happy, for everybody that lives has something to bear which he would prefer to be without, since suffering is universal and it embraces all mankind—the good as well as the bad, the saint as well as the sinner—and so our only solace in this life is to look forward to the day

32 / *The Holy Dybbuk*

when we shall be blessedly released from this life and be where no sorrow of any kind will every be able to reach us.

Sounds like a Sunday sermon, but I know you won't mind being preached to along these lines. . . .

Charlie

June 20, 1961

Dear Ronda,

. . . . Keep on fighting the "good fight" both against your own passions and every other obstacle which will be placed between your own soul and the inconceivable Beauty of Christ's Being. Remember, Ronda, He is the most beautiful among the sons of men and there will never be any human being you will meet in this life that can equal His goodness and love for a person like you. We are all sinners; even the holiest person who has ever lived is unclean in God's sight. So keep this thought in your mind so that you may know that you are loved and cherished by the Immortal One who is Christ the Lord.

Oh how I wish I could state in words the extent of Christ's love for the likes of you. But I cannot. Only in the next life will you fully realize how ardent God's love has been for you and how He values and cherishes your soul. The Holy Scriptures are full of expressions of God's love for people like you, but I can't quote them to you for lack of space. "I have loved you with an everlasting love," is one of these.

Men love us with a love that is finite and limited, but the love of God for us is without bounds. Think of this, for such a thought is enough to make a saint of the most hardened sinner.

Love God, Ronda, and you will be happy in time and eternity. Love Him because He loves you and does so every single instant of the day, for every instant of the day His concern for your well-being is such that in His eyes you are the only person that exists. He wants you one hundred percent. He wants to clasp you close to His Sacred Heart, so don't pull away or resist His manifestations of affection for you which are present in everything that exists, for in everything that exists there is written these words for you: "I, the Lord of Creation, love you." He is always saying this to you personally and He does so by everything that occurs.

Charlie

Letters of Charles Rich / 33

July 11, 1961

Dear Ronda,

. . . It's very nice of you to feel so concerned about a congenial place for me to be in and live the kind of life I do, but God has other designs and it's His will in the matter that really counts. [*Charlie thought he would have to leave the Jesuit house, and it was of great concern to him. Although it took quite a long time for things to be straightened out, in the end he didn't have to move.*—Ed.]

. . . I have always realized that due to the fact I have to live the kind of spiritual life I do, I can have no guarantee how or in what environment I will end up my days, and, as Fr. Raphael Simon once said to me, I "have God for my security," and, believe me, that's security enough for any man.

There are quite a few words in the psalms which in Hebrew signify "safety," "security," and "well-being," and which same can only be had from God. "You are my security," the sweet singer of Israel is every once in awhile saying to God, and he does so in many different kinds of words signifying the same thing.

In this age in which the craze for security is so overwhelming and the lack of it so prominent in the lives of men, it's good to take the words of the Psalmist to heart and to do what he does whenever he feels lonely and uncertain as to what will happen to him in this life.

"God," the Psalmist keeps on saying to us today, "is well able to care and to provide for our every need both material and spiritual," so it's to Him we should go when the thought of what will happen to us in the future presents itself to our mind. "Cast your cares upon the Lord and He will sustain you."

I myself have been doing this for the past twenty-nine years in the Church since I have all this time had to depend on the charity of my friends for my daily sustenance. Somebody has to live by faith and so it's a privilege to be chosen for such a purpose.

I don't say we shouldn't be provident and make preparation for our future material needs. But in my case, it is definitely the will of God that I should live from day to day and be completely dependent upon His divine providence in my regard. And while it's been extraordinarily nice and wonderful and convenient to have been able to have spent

34 / *The Holy Dybbuk*

thirteen years of my life in a Jesuit environment, still, it may be better for me spiritually to do without the advantages to be had here.

And so, realizing that God knows better than I do what is or what is not good for me from the angle of the life to come, I ask for the grace to leave myself completely in His hands and be as though I did not exist, that is, totally devoid of my own will and to have His will become my will.

Will you help me pray that this should be perfectly accomplished for the few remaining years I will have to stay in this world? Thank you, not only for this but for every other good holy thought you have ever had for me.

Keep yourself cheerful and you will conquer the battles of life since it's only by means of a holy kind of joy in the substance of the soul that this can be done. "Rejoice," St. Paul is always saying to those he loves. And how often does not this word "joy" occur in the psalms, indicating that a cheerful spirit is the one thing necessary on the road to high holiness?

Charlie

July 29, 1961

Dear Ronda,

...I consider it an almost sacred duty to reply to anyone who is willing to go to the trouble of writing....

As you by now realize, I am at one of the turning points in my life as a Catholic because, after living in a religious community for thirteen years, a great adjustment will have to be made to live with a private family. With this in view, I count on your prayers that, if it's God's will and good for my eternal well-being, some place should turn up like my former residence where I could spend the rest of my earthly life. I know only too well that we can never know what is or what is not good for us in a spiritual way, and so we must leave the final outcome of all things in the hands of Divine Providence, and this I intend to do in this particular matter.

Still, it is at the same time equally pleasing to God if we hope for great things from the hands of one Who is so infinitely and so

Letters of Charles Rich / 35

Supremely Great. Our Lord Himself tells us to do this very thing when He says, "Ask and you shall receive." He does not put any limitations on our requests and so we should not do so either. We should ask for the impossible from Him to whom nothing is impossible, provided we do so in the proper Christian way, that is, perfectly resigned to God's holy will.

. . . Go to the saints, Ronda, if you want to really know what heaven is like, because they have actually been there as the result of the extraordinary graces they, for reasons known to themselves, received from God. The saints come closer to God than any other group of people because they actually touched "the hem of His garment." Nobody would ever have any difficulty with matters of faith if he only would let himself be influenced by the lives of the saints and permit their spirit and their approach to things Divine to impregnate his soul.

The first thing I myself did as soon as I was baptized was to soak myself in the lives of the saints and let their views dominate my life. There is a four volume Lives of the Saints which you ought to read in the same way as you do the Holy Scriptures, for these books are equally important for the purpose of getting to know and love God. They are published by Kenedy and Sons, New York.

The saints were God's most intimate friends and so He communicated a sort of special knowledge of Himself to them which He withholds from those who are not saints. And so associating ourselves with them we become sharers in this knowledge and receive some of God's secrets, the secrets of love the Song of Songs speaks about. Who else but a great saint could tell us the things St. Ignatius Loyola said, or St. Teresa? If you let yourself become an intimate friend of the saints, you will receive a knowledge of God to be had in no other way, and a lot of problems that disturb others will not exist for you, for God will be so real for you that you will take Him for granted as you do your own existence and the whole universe.

. . . The main thing is to love God, Ronda, since if you do this to your dying day, heaven and all that's there is yours.

Charlie

36 / *The Holy Dybbuk*

August 11, 1961

Dear Ronda,

...I am getting old and as I think about it I am tempted to be afraid. I am not afraid because I am getting old, but because as the years slip away the prospect of facing God face to face is getting closer and closer, and who would not be concerned at facing God in His unveiled presence?

All the saints were a little bit holily afraid in this respect and they did not hesitate to say so. It's nothing wrong to be afraid in a holy way, for that kind of fear does not, in the least way, take away our peace and our confidence in the goodness and mercy and love of our Father in heaven and His only Begotten Son.

It's one thing to look forward to meeting God when we are still far off from the prospect of doing so, but as we get on in years, death takes on a reality it did not have when we were young.

We need grace to be prepared for the Feast Day our soul will experience when it is loosed from the flesh to which it has so long been so mysteriously united, and there is a passage in one of the prophets which says: "Be prepared, O Israel, to meet thy God."

Still, there is nothing to worry about, because when the time comes for us to die, we will receive God's special help and so what now seems so strange will then become easy and familiar, for we will pass out of this world in the same way as when we came into it, that is, in the arms of our loving Father in Heaven with the Blessed Virgin nearby and all the angels and saints to assist our doing so....

In Corde Jesu,

Charlie

August 31, 1961

Dear Ronda,

...We are living in Apocalyptic times and so it's a great opportunity for high holiness. It seems that God has no other way of letting us know the utter worthlessness of things that have to pass away and so He is allowing the world to fall into its present misery—the Russians

Letters of Charles Rich / 37

just announced that they will resume their tests and this means that the whole earth will face contamination from them.

In dealing with Communism, you are confronted with the most diabolical forces that have ever appeared on this earth, for in order to maintain the doctrines of Marx and Lenin, the Communists were willing to destroy the earth. Lenin said that even if he had to kill off three-fourths of the human race in order to establish his nefarious doctrines, he would not hesitate to do so, and I wonder what such evil-minded men as he have to face when they confront the Almighty. It must be terrible for a Stalin or a Krushev [sic] to have to account for the atrocities they committed or which were countenanced by them. We can't judge what will happen to them.

Communism is a proof that the mystery of evil will always be with us, for we cannot figure out why there should be so much suffering on this earth and why God should allow murderers like these to accomplish what they do. Anyway, this world has never been a bed of roses and it never will be. Maybe God wants this truth to become clear in the minds of men and so He allows the Communists to grow and flourish.

It's not the first time in human history in which such cataclysmic events as those now taking place have occurred, for if you read the Old Testament, you will see that God allowed the Jewish kingdom to be entirely destroyed and the people to be enslaved in captivity by their cruel masters, such as the Persians and Babylonians.

The same thing is taking place today and we are again witnessing the evils of old in which suffering and slavery was so widespread. It's good to reflect as to why God lets this take place, for it makes us realize that He wants us to take refuge in the hope of a completely other life in which what we have to suffer now will no longer exist.

God, as it were, has to force us to love Him, and so He allows the world to disintegrate before our eyes. "Is this the kind of world to which you so attach your hearts?" He seems to be saying to us. There is nothing here worth regretting having to leave and the author of the Book of Ecclesiastes tells us this when he says "Vanity of vanities, all is vanity." These are not the words of a pessimist but of one who sees things as they are and so he is able to place the things of this life in their proper perspective.

38 / *The Holy Dybbuk*

This age will probably go down in history as one of the most violent we have ever known. Still, for those who love God, He, God, makes even the evils we now experience work for the good of those who love Him—at least that's what St. Paul maintains and we with him.

It's a great opportunity to aim for great things and so we should thank God even for the evils we now go through, for from the angle of the life to come they are our greatest blessing....

Charlie

September 13, 1961

Dear Ronda,

I can't help but admire the promptness with which you keep up your end of the correspondence and so I have to do mine. I forgot to answer the question you asked in your last letter as to what I think of the Life of Christ by Francois Mauriac. The only thing I can say to most of the lives of Christ I have ever read is that they don't help me much as regards getting an idea of Who and What He is. The only life of Christ that has been able to do this are the passages in the Old Testament referring to Him by way of Figure and Type and especially as they are found expressed in the Song of Songs.

I have been greatly helped in that direction by everything I have read referring to Him in the Fathers and Doctors of the Church as well as in the writings of the saints. St. Thomas Aquinas has written two volumes along this line, and though they are a little dry to read, the doctrinal exposition of all Christ is, is indispensable.

Then you have another and equally remarkable Life of Christ by the greatest mind of the Church since Thomas Aquinas—namely Franciscus Suarez. I have read his two volumes on this subject in a Spanish translation and find them the most complete and learned account of Our Lord in all literature, outside the Scriptures, as well as one of the deepest and most sublime of them.

But, as to authors like Mauriac, I simply can't get used to the idea of reading their works in reference to a subject for which so much learning and holiness is required in order to be able to write about. But my main dependence for knowledge of Our Lord is of course the Gospels and Epistles of St. Paul and the cultivation of a deep intimate

Letters of Charles Rich / 39

relationship with Him by means of prayer and contemplation, for it's through prayer alone that most of our knowledge of Christ can be acquired. By prayer, of course, I mean the entire spiritual and interior life, for when we pray in the right way something of the wonder and beauty of the Personality of Christ is infused into our soul that cannot be had in any other way.

When we pray and mortify our inner being, like our judgment and our will, we acquire a facility which enables us to become intimately united to Our Divine Lord and have a knowledge of Him that cannot be expressed in words. Love, properly practiced, is the best way to get to know Christ and I have so far found no substitute for it. By love I mean what the Scripture does when it makes use of that word, that is, not something sentimental, but an exercise that involves our entire being as it is at present, composed of both body and mind, intellect and will.

If we love Christ with our whole hearts, with our minds and with the strength of everything in us, we will soon be able to acquire a knowledge of Christ so sublime and transcendent that we would not want it to be expressed in any word we can use, nor would we have to do such a thing, for in heaven we will know Christ so intimately that we will stand in no need of having to express the knowledge of Him in any known medium.

We can, even in this life, with the help of God's grace, acquire such deep and intimate acquaintanceship with Our Divine Lord that we will feel no need to put the nature of it into any kind of expression. You may call this a kind of mystical grace such as mostly all the saints possessed, and of which same St. Teresa of Avila speaks with such facility and such sublime beauty.

St. Teresa, and those like her, had a knowledgeless knowledge of Christ which they would not even think of trying to communicate to any other person because there is no way in which this can be done. She speaks about this knowledge of Christ in her *Autobiography* so it's there for anyone to read. She speaks especially of the beauty of the whiteness of Christ's hands, and when you read it you are convinced she saw what few others had been privileged to do. St. Paul also saw Christ in this way and had a knowledge of Him no words could ever

40 / *The Holy Dybbuk*

succeed in trying to communicate to anyone else who did not share his own experience.

It's this knowledge of Christ that I have always asked God to have, for it's this knowledge of Him that can alone satisfy the soul's craving for him on this earth.

You can see from this that men like Mauriac won't have much influence over me, for I long to know Christ as all the saints have done and do what they did in order to acquire such knowledge.

Every day we hear of men who have become outstanding in the particular fields in which they are so busily engaged. We hear of men who are outstanding in the field of medicine or chemistry or physics or in the different arts. But we can also become outstanding in the love and knowledge of Our Divine Lord and become masters in His own divine science. We can acquire a knowledge of Christ that makes all other fields of learning dull and uninteresting.

When you read the references to Christ made by the Fathers and Doctors of the Church, you find them to be so overwhelming that no other writers can satisfy you, and in this respect I have particularly in mind the two-volume commentary on the Gospel of St. John by St. Cyril of Alexandria which is nothing else but a life of Christ in the strict sense of the word. I have read and re-read this enormous work over and over again and the more I do so, the more convinced I am that it cannot be equalled by other authors. It would take at least a dozen years to do this work justice and I myself have actually spent that time on it. This is the only kind of life of Christ that has done me any good and which has taught me things about Our Lord I could have found out in no other way. Personally, I think it's one of the greatest lives of Christ ever written and which, if read with care and study, would entice the soul with a knowledge of Christ you would not think possible to attain in this life.

. . . I look back on my twenty-nine years in the Church and see the enormous amount of things you can learn in all that time. When I do this I think of St. Ignatius Loyola who compared his first years of his conversion from a worldly life to the "kindergarten stage." This is the way he described his first years of prayer life.

When I first became a Catholic, I actually prayed that God should

Letters of Charles Rich / 41

take me out of the world, for I had such a craving to be with Him in Heaven. This prayer—with the permission of my director—lasted for many years. I now see why God saw fit to answer it in His own way because of the enormous amount of knowledge of Himself I have since acquired, for we learn an awful lot about Christ as the years accumulate we could have found out in no other way. You too will find this to be the case the longer you stay in the Church and so when you will look back to the first five or ten years you, too, will call them the "kindergarten stage" of your interior and spiritual life.

In fact, the only really good reason for living is to get to know Christ better, because this can only be accomplished with the passage of time. Time will teach you things about Christ you could have found out in no other way, so welcome the coming years as a means to this. You will learn an awful lot the longer you will stay in the Church and that will be the compensating factor of your life, filled as the years will be with sufferings which no man can avoid.

So be cheerful as you look ahead to the years yet to come for they will bring with them a knowledge and love for Our Divine Lord to be had in no other way. . . .

Charlie

October 4, 1961

Dear Ronda,

. . . It must have been very enjoyable to have had your sister with you, and I am sure the impression she received will remain in her and will be of spiritual help in her quest for the truth that St. Francis loved so much and to the spread of which he was so ardently devoted. [*My sister Carla came to Italy to visit me and she was most impressed by Assisi. Later she converted to the Catholic faith as well.*—Ed.]

It's only the Church that produces a St. Francis of Assisi, whom Pope Pius XI called the greatest person that has appeared on this earth. I read the "Little Flowers of St. Francis" long before I ever thought of being a Catholic, and when I did I felt myself entering into a brand new world. This was my first taste of Christian spirituality and it won my heart completely over to itself. I guess I was not the only one to discover Christ so beautifully relived in the life of this Saint.

42 / The Holy Dybbuk

I had many influences working on my soul prior to its entry into the Church, and Franciscan spirituality constituted an important one of these, for, like the writings of St. Augustine and the other Fathers of the Church, they helped fill up the void in my inner being.

I know one Franciscan Father who has the reputation of being an undoubted saint and it's been a source of consolation for me to have known him so well for about twenty-five years. When I first met him, he told me that since he was a boy his ambition was to live in this century the same kind of life as St. Francis did in his own age. According to everyone who knows him, including many Franciscan Fathers, he has succeeded pretty well in this aim, for he really and truly is another St. Francis of Assisi. Fr. John Francis Granahan is now in Brazil and when he first got there he was marked for death, because he denounced publically the scandalous life of the mayor of the town he was in. A trap was set for him when he was summoned to a sick call, but his death was avoided when another Father in the house went in his stead. After beating this priest almost to death, they realized that they had the wrong man and let him go. When I asked Fr. John about the incident, his answer was that he was not worthy of the grace of martyrdom.

From this you can see that I have some deep interest in Franciscanism, and that its spirit had even before my conversion made deep inroads into my life, inroads that helped me find the sweet, loving truth Our Divine Lord is.

. . . In praising so much the Fathers and Doctors of the Church, I did not mean to cast aspersions on the writers of the present day, for I have in the past twenty-nine years read more than my share of them and gotten a great deal out of what I read.

. . . I am praying for you that you should grow and flourish in the faith. . . for after you will be in it around fifteen or twenty years, you will begin to realize how wonderful it is and what a grace that you should be chosen by God out of so many vast millions to be incorporated into it.

Don't forget to thank God each day that you are a Catholic, for that is the best way to obtain the grace of final perseverance, for without this last grace all others we receive are in vain. But to get the grace to

Letters of Charles Rich / 43

remain in the Church is just as important as to be able to enter into it, and St. Augustine says that some people get the grace of conversion without getting the grace to persevere in the faith. Why, he says, we do not know. But the fact remains that this is so, and so we must pray continually for the grace of final perseverance and do all in our power to dispose our souls for such a grace.

St. Augustine says that to get the grace of final perseverance, we must pray as long as we live; we must do so every single day of our lives, and if you read Goethe's *Faust*, you will find there a passage which says the same thing. Only that person, Goethe says, is deserving of his freedom—like his existence—who daily wins it anew. It's dangerous to take anything for granted, and so we must make acts of appreciation of the fact that we have the grace to be members of the true Church.

I am sorry for these sermon-like few words. But after being over twenty-nine years in the Church, I am only now beginning to realize that it's only due to God's goodness and love and to His infinite mercy that I am still in it, for every day someone who was once blessed with the gift of the true faith finds himself away from it.

It's a great grace to be able to spend such a long time in the Church, for we in that way get to know better as to all that God is. We can never get to know Him too well, but every little bit of knowledge concerning Him Who we love so much is an added way to grow and increase in this love, for the more the mind knows, the more the heart loves; "as we see," one saint said, "so do we love."

. . . That's all for just now, so goodby in all that's beautiful, good, and true.

Charlie

October 15, 1961

Dear Ronda,

It's time for you not to be so concerned with your relationship with God but with God Himself. God does not want us to have any kind of anxiety whatever as to what He thinks of us, but to completely forget ourselves altogether and think only of Him. For in His eyes it does not matter what we are, whether good or bad, virtuous or not: what does

44 / The Holy Dybbuk

matter and that *greatly* is that we think of Him and not of our relationship with Him.

Throw yourself completely away and then you will find yourself marvelously in Him. Don't be concerned whether or not you are close to Him, but be concerned *about* Him. For God Himself will make up for your lack of love or closeness to Him. Christ is good, He is Holy, and so it does not matter whether you are good or whether you are holy. What matters is that you should find your whole consolation in the fact that He is Divine and All-Good and All-Beautiful and All-Virtuous, that is all. Christ will make up for all your deficiencies and so why worry? Be a little holily reckless, holily selfless, holily careless about everything and just rest in the lap of the Divine Son of God, for that pleases Christ and nothing else. He wants us to be like a little child without a worry or care in the world.... We are holy and perfect in the holiness and perfection of Christ and so it's a complete waste of time to be concerned or anxious whether we are holy or whether we are perfect, for that is what St. Augustine means when he says: "Love God and do what you will."

..."Worry and trouble are for hell; the children of God ought not to know them." Engrave these words of Venerable Libermann on your heart and mind and all the things you complain about in your letters will completely disappear. There is another saying of his, equally important and helpful: "Jesus and Mary do not wish to be feared; they wish to be *loved*....

Charlie

November 1, 1961

Dear Ronda,

...It's incredible to what extremes the saints go to make known their intense craving for the life to come, "O life," St. Teresa says, "who are the enemy of all my Good, would it were lawful to end thee."

You'll find these words in her famous *Exclamations*. Read them all through and they'll thrill you beyond expression. It's for this reason I have been so fond of St. Bernard's *Commentary on the Song of Songs*, for he always talks there of the joys of heaven and makes little of those there are on this earth. The joys of earth are good only because they

Letters of Charles Rich / 45

give us a slight taste of the ones we shall one day have in the life to come, and no one has written more sweetly of these joys than he.

St. Bernard has done more for my soul than any other saint I ever prayed to, because his writings on the Song of Songs became like a pair of wings on which my soul was able to soar into the regions of inner bliss. It was St. Bernard more than anyone else who made me acquainted with the divine sweetness to be found in the Human Nature of Our Divine Lord.... St. Bernard had inner visions of the beauty of Christ's Being and how sweet and loveable that Being was....

In brief, St. Bernard is "tops" as we say in our modern jargon, but it's a good word to describe him in. I know of no one in the Church, outside of Sacred Scriptures, my soul owes so much to, and so my love for him is naturally unbounded....

Your dear friend in Him,

Charlie

November 13, 1961

Dear Ronda,

It was a delight to hear about Carla, and we should all pray for her to get the grace to make whatever sacrifice her entry into the Church may require. There has to be sacrifice in anything that's worthwhile, and so, no matter how easy the transition may appear from error to truth, it does require some effort of mind and heart with which this can be done.

I have now been—or will be this coming March—thirty years in the Church, and if there is anything a person so much older in it than you can say to you, it is that the longer one remains in the Church, the more penetrated with its truth and beauty the soul becomes. The Church, Ronda, is Christ, for "Christ and the Church," St. Gregory the Great tells us, "constitutes one Person." The Church is Christ and Christ is the Church, and "he who has not the Church for a Mother cannot have God for a Father." These last words are not mine but those of St. Cyprian who had the grace to lay down his life for the principle that the Church and Christ constitute one Person.

46 / *The Holy Dybbuk*

And what do we mean by the Church, we may further inquire? The answer to this question is given in the penny catechism, and so there is no need to say anything further on this matter.

. . . Once this truth is firmly fixed in the soul, the problems a convert may have are for the most part solved. They are solved by the fact that for him there can only be one road to eternal happiness and it is the one on which he has been placed by God by the grace of conversion. . . .

It is too bad so many people find old age so burdensome to bear, for if they did what they could when they were young, they would welcome growing old as an opportunity to grow in the love for things divine, for these are more appreciated with the growing years and they mellow in the soul like rare wine. Things spiritual are much better appreciated and valued by the soul when we are older than when we are young, for as the passions become more disciplined, the light from heaven has a better chance to illuminate our interior being and fill it with the joy thereof.

It's interesting to think that the word "light" in Hebrew is a synonym for "joy" and so the more light from heaven there is in the depths of the soul, the more its happiness increases, for they grow in direct proportion to one another. Pray that this light from heaven may enter your own soul and illuminate it with the Beauty of Christ; and Christ is beautiful, Ronda, since the Psalmist refers to Him as "fairer in beauty you are than the sons of men" (Ps. 44:3). And who does not recall the words of the Song of Songs in this respect, for we are there told that He is "A flower of Sharon and a lily of the valley. Ah, you are beautiful, my lover, yes, you are lovely."

What wonderful words with which to address Christ! It's too bad we do not use this song to make known our love for things divine, for the recitation of them would fill our heart with a joy from heaven. It's significant that this song is still used by the Jews as a liturgical hymn on the Passover, and so this is a clear proof that its meaning is sacred, divine, and not human alone, for the Song of Songs speaks of the Beauty of the Son of God and of the soul's love for Him and of His for the soul.

Well, Ronda, I don't know what else to say to you, so keep up the good fight of which St. Paul speaks as he refers to the struggle we have to make to keep our hearts full of the things of the next life. We have to strive for what's of a nature never to have an end, and that's why we have to wage such warfare on this earth, for there are many hidden foes to the aspirations of our higher nature and so they seek to drag us down to what is finite and perishable.

It's for things infinite we have been made and the poet Goethe has a beautiful passage in reference to this which I'll quote in its original, hoping you'll get someone to give you some sort of proper explanation for it in English: *Nicht sum verganglichen/ Wie aus gesha!/ Uns zu verewigen/ Sind wir ja da.* In my poor German this means we are here to eternalize ourselves and we do not exist in this life for the passing things or good to be found in it. It's a magically beautiful line in German, but our English cannot do it justice. We are here to become capable of having eternal life in ourselves for "ewigkeit" means eternity in that language. We are not here for the sake of passing goods or for whatever takes place in this life, Goethe tells us, and Christianity confirms his statement.

What a grace it is to be able to base the actions of our life on the principle that we shall all soon be in heaven and that heaven actually exists and that we have the grace to be able to believe that this is so. Many lack that grace, and so we have to have gratitude to God that we are spared from such a fate—that of not having the grace to be able to believe all the Church teaches in reference to the life to come.

Many saints had this faith in the form of a mystical experience of God which assured them beyond the power to doubt that there is something immortal about themselves, for so convinced were they of the truths of faith, that, if the Bible had never been written, and the Church never existed, they would have believed everything they do by the experience they had of these truths.

. . . The day is bound to come when you will turn to holiness of life as the sole solution to any problem that can come up in this life as far as you are concerned. . . . and I shall pray to God that you should indeed become a saint.

Goodbye,

Charlie

How about praying for me once in a while? I always do so for you and will keep it up till you won't need them any more.

48 / *The Holy Dybbuk*

[*Soon after this I got married and first moved back to New York City, and then to Spring Valley in Rockland, near New York City. But there was a little strain during this time because I felt that Charlie was disappointed that I was going to marry. He had thought I would make a fine contemplative nun. When I actually met him in New York City, however, he said that if God had joined Martin and me together in marriage, that was proof it was not God's will for me to be a nun, and he was happy to know me as a married woman and wanted to get to know Martin also. My husband, who came from a very similar orthodox Jewish background like Charlie's, took an immediate liking to Charlie and considered him to be one of the most authentic Catholics he had met. But we only saw him occasionally after the move to Rockland.*

When still in New York City, I would have liked to see Charlie more frequently, but he was always careful not to overdo visiting with people, lest he take time and concentration away from his life of prayer. But it was always, for me, a great treat to visit with him, and my little twin-daughters found him delightful. They used to sit on his lap and pat his head and go into giggling fits over him, which I thought wild and unmanageable then, but now, twenty-four years later, think was charming of them.

This sequence, then, begins in 1967 when I was in Rockland, New York, and Charlie in New York City.—Ed.]

Undated

Dear Ronda,

. . . I would like to write you a long letter, but the days of doing so are over as far as I am concerned. I no longer have the satisfaction I used to in the written word, since it is exceeded infinitely in the one that is spoken face to face. I am also kind of impatient with the finitude of things and the limited way there is of communicating our thoughts and feelings in the present life. In brief, I am impatient with time and long for eternity with the amplitude of life we will there experience.

Letters of Charles Rich / 49

However, I am at the same time willing to stay here if that would be of any benefit to my neighbor.

There are a few thoughts this morning which I would like you to dwell on, for they alone would make you the saint you so earnestly strive to become. Here they are—they are taken from the writing of a saint whose name I forgot:

"The truth and light of the soul is nothing else but God. I beg you to be full of gaiety. Oh! how much it is needed by people of good will. This gaiety is willed by God. We ought to honor it in the Heart of Our Lord and strive to draw it to ourselves. Honor the gaiety of Our Lord's Heart—keep it wholly cheerful and in so doing honor the holy calm of Our Lord." . . .

Charlie

May 7, 1968

Dear Ronda,

. . . There has been a little news in regard to myself, externally speaking, because a few weeks ago I found out I had a slightly torn retina in my right eye and other complications. It is being treated at the eye clinic. It is doubtful when it will clear up or whether I won't have to have surgery.

I was sixty-nine years old last month—at least legally speaking. There is no sure date as to my birth, but my naturalization papers state I was born April 22, 1899. It comforts me to think I am so old because it means less time to do on earth and the sooner to enter heaven. I still need prayers, though, in order to get there, so I count on you for them.

There is really no end or beginning to what I would like to tell you since it concerns that which is endless. I have always—even long before I entered the Church—tried to live with the thought of eternity in my mind and so I was glad to learn that even Neitzsche could say: Ich liebe dich, O Ewigkeit (I love thee, O eternity). But now that I have the grace to love the Truth made Flesh, it is inexpressible to tell the joy my heart feels at the thought I shall soon "go up to the house of the Lord," as the Psalmist puts it.

. . . Now with this eye complication, there are other prospects of the

50 / *The Holy Dybbuk*

cross and it all goes to assure me of God's love in my regard, for He could have spared me on earth and so deprived me of the merit a little suffering out of love for Him would have procured and the effects of that merit for all eternity.

We should not be over-concerned as to what happens to us in this life, for good or bad. God can turn it to our greater spiritual and eternal good. This is the attitude I have in reference to my present physical condition and the doctor told me that what happened to one eye can also happen to the other—in other words, there is a prospect of not one day being able to see in them both. [*He had successful surgery and is now able to read well.*—Ed.]

I don't know why I write this way to you, but perhaps I don't know what else to say, and I do like to say something to you, and do so out of love for God. The soul gets so full of God that it cannot contain itself and so at the slightest opportunity it bursts forth with words in reference to that love, though what it is trying to say is so difficult to express.

I know you love God very much, so I am telling you He gave me a little cross to assure me I will one day go to heaven. It's all right to pray and meditate and contemplate, but there is nothing like a little suffering to asure us that God has our eternal interests at heart and that He has no intention to forsake us along that line. . . .

Charlie

July 31, 1968

Dear Ronda,

Thanks for your long and encouraging letter. God sent you out there [California] to become a saint and you will do this by weeping for the Church and the many Judases she has in her fold in the persons of her false priests and, as you say, heretical theologians, or even cowardly ones. Imagine one of them telling people to disobey the Holy Father in his pronouncements on birth control, and which same comes from the teaching authority of the Church and her magisterium. I believe the devil uses these so-called theologians and makes them perform his nefarious tasks.

Letters of Charles Rich / 51

There is never a lack of devils, St. John of the Cross says, to overthrow the saints. You are a saint, and if you think you are not, then do all you can to become one. You will convert Martin by means of your sanctity and nothing else. He does not need arguments, but the sight of your own loving self, and as that self is so completely committed to the love for things divine, and as these things are embodied in the Person of Our Lord.

These are momentous days, and historians will point out they were necessary to produce saints. What if millions leave the Church? Is this not a blessing in disguise, since by ridding herself of those who will prove disloyal to her directives, those who remain will shine forth with greater brilliance. It all happens for the sake of the saints and no other reason—it's them God wants and not millions of half-hearted lovers.

. . . I was glad to read of your love for the Holy Father, and I am sure God will reward you for it beyond all expectations. Thank God for the grace you have to love Him so much and to love Him in the persons of those whom He has set over His Church.

. . . I am getting tired of the written word because, compared to the spoken one, it is so pale and ineffectual. Years ago, I thought differently, but as time goes on, I can see why the greatest things that have ever been said were said by word of mouth. Moses did not write to Aaron, he spoke to him. And so did St. Paul to those with whom he lived. I am not against writing because it was used by the greatest saints and doctors of the Church. However, my preference, as I go on living, is for the spoken word. . . .

Your dear friend,

Charlie

. . . The doctors at St. Vincent's informed me I have diabetes and it's this disease which caused all the eye damage. There is little to be done except dieting, and that I can't keep too well on account of the irregular way of my life from a physical point of view. [*He means eating whatever is served in the Residence, which is good, but not diet food.*—Ed.]

I am ready to meet God face to face and so I am thankful to Him for giving me the grace to long to be dissolved and to be with Christ.

52 / *The Holy Dybbuk*

...There is a beautiful expression in one of the prophetical books which reads "Be prepared to meet thy God, O Israel." Israel, of course, here means every believing person.

December 21, 1968

Dear Ronda,

I hope this gets to you in time for the Christmas joys and of which same I wish you an unlimited supply. I shall continue praying for Martin, but let God decide the best way there is of making him His very own. These ways have no beginning and no end, and as St. Francis de Sales says, "There are as many different kinds of sanctities as there are saints."

Years ago I acted in a very narrow and stupid way when it came to try to get people to love the God I loved so much. But with experience, I realize that God Himself is the best one to judge how anyone should come to Him. I still of course believe that there is only one true way of getting there, but there are also unnumbered amounts of people who are in the one true Church without their realizing it.

This morning I watched the space missile take off and as I did so I realized of how little importance such an event is compared with the inner world of inexpressible wealth with which the soul of the most humble of us is filled, and how much more adventurous it is to set out on our journey to heaven by becoming a saint before we get there. I also reflected on the fact that the great saints never made too much of discoveries like those of Christopher Columbus, and that those who were his contemporaries never alluded to them or to the discoveries. This indicates that it's the inner world alone that counts and that it is that world which is alone real and true and genuine. I am getting into your sphere [philosophy] now so I'd better be careful. [*I recall disagreeing with Charlie here—I found the walk on the moon extraordinarily exciting. But in October 1984, after re-reading these lines, Charlie wrote to say that he agreed that the moon walk was tremendously exciting.—Ed.*]

...I still miss having you close by, but that won't be for too long since it's only a breath of air between time and eternity. The Hebrew

Letters of Charles Rich / 53

for vanity is "a breath of air," and that's what the Psalmist says everything mortal is.

I thank God for giving me this passion for what's of a nature to last forever.

Charlie

February 22, 1969

Dear Ronda,

...In reference to the many weaknesses which so many saints had and which in no way detracted from the holiness of their lives, there is a passage in the book of Judges that has direct bearing along this line. The words have a historical sense, but this in no way prevents us from applying them to the way God works in the souls of His saints. Here they are: "Because this people have transgressed my convenant...and have not obeyed my voice, I will not henceforth drive out before them any of the nations that Joshua left when he died, that by them I may test Israel, whether they will take care to walk in the way of the Lord.... So the Lord left those nations, not driving them out at once, and he did not give them into the power of Joshua" (Judges 2:20-23).

This passage throws a lot of light on the way God treats those He loves very much like yourself. For He permits them to have many weaknesses so that they may have something to fight against all their life long, as well as to trust that in spite of these weaknesses He loves them very much, even as a devoted mother loves a child that has many failings. We should in no way worry about our failings and should say with St. Francis de Sales: "Dear imperfections," for it is these very imperfections that call down God's mercy on us as well as His infinite compassion. The weaker we are the more we feel ourselves in need of His mercy, and so in this way grow in love and gratitude.

Well, Ronda, goodbye and give my love to Martin and the girls.

Charlie

August 26, 1969

Dear Ronda,

...St. Teresa said when we get to heaven we will see that we owe more to the sinner than to the saint, and I agree wholeheartedly with her. I have always felt that misplaced action and behavior inspire others to go in the opposite direction and so all these defections will impel those who love God to go out of their way to show their loyalty to him and thus become saints. You are among these people, and that's why so much is expected of you. You came into the Church at the right time, for it now gives you a chance to make up for the love so many withhold from God. You have to compensate Him for this love, and so far you have done a very good job. Keep it up....

Charlie

September 28, 1969

Dear Ronda,

A Franciscan friar once said to St. Catherine of Genoa that he was in a higher state than herself, hinting at the fact that she on that account can't be as close to God as he was, to which words St. Catherine replied as follows: "That you are in a higher state I grant you, but you will never make me believe that I can't love God as much as you do. If I knew that I could love God more than I do with your habit on, I would tear it off your back and put it on."

I think this ought to settle your mind at rest as to the celibate state. With God's grace, we can be anything we sincerely desire which we find in accordance with the highest type of sanctity. There have been married women who were the recipients of the sublimest mystical graces, like Blessed Maria Taigi. She had seven children to take care of, when one day Our Lord appeared to her in church and told her to go home to attend to her duties there. This was a genuine vision authenticated by the Church's authority and not something she imagined. The main thing is love, as St. Augustine says, for then we can both *do* and *be* what we will. When you appear before Our Lord in heaven, you won't be able to say to Him that you were unable to become a saint because of your married state....

It will interest you to know that prior to my conversion, I was a deep admirer of the writings of Plotinus and read them with deep devotion. He was one of the steps to where God has now brought my soul, so I

Letters of Charles Rich / 55

have to be grateful for the help to heaven I then got from him.

. . . I am also very happy to hear the good news about Martin and do hope he will ultimately find what his heart has been longing for so long without suspecting it—Christ. It looks to me that God is finally drawing him close to Himself, so that you can now have the hope of both of you being happy together when you are both in the Beatific state.

A few days ago I received a letter from Tom Prendergast, who is also one of your admirers and who Fr. Somerville, his director, said "is one of the finest souls I have ever met." This Tom wrote these words to me: "I want to say something about your writings, but I don't know what to say, except that after reading most of these writings it seems to me that you yourself, according to these same writings, are on the threshold of heaven and the next step is inside. At the same time, they are helping me to arrive or be on the same beautiful and glorious threshold."

I have always considered Tom a real saint of God because of the heroic manner in which he practices the Christian virtues of faith, hope, and charity. I know of no one who, were he in his position, would not be tempted to despair on account of the terrible and humiliating sufferings he has for the past twenty years been through. [*These sufferings are related to severe incurable ailments.*—Ed.]

I see him on the average of every two weeks, because he is in no position to come to see me, and every time I do so I leave with a peace of soul no other person I know could leave with me. Tom is the most joyous and the most truly Christlike peaceful soul I now know, and it's a blessing to be with him for the time that I am.

I have read the lives of hundreds upon hundreds of saints that the Church has officially declared as such, and his own life parallels any of them. His main contribution to the well-being of the mystical body of Christ is the way he bears all he has to and the deep peace and joy of spirit these sufferings produce in him. When you leave him you have the impresion you have been with a saint.

I often feel that it's a waste of time to write all I do, but when I see Tom and he tells me all the help his soul receives from them, I feel compensated for all the trouble these writings cause. With St. Augus-

56 / *The Holy Dybbuk*

tine, I feel I'd rather read what someone else writes about God than to do so myself.

...St. Teresa says that it is perfectly pleasing to God to want to become a great saint.

...I guess I better stop because I am starting to ramble on. Goodbye till I hear from you again and don't stop praying for one who is always praying for you and who will not stop doing so till we shall both meet each other in heaven.

Your very very dear friend in Him we both have the grace to love so much,

Charlie

April, 1970

Dear Ronda,

Last week I was seventy-one, and so the thought of heaven is getting very real to me, more so than it has ever been since my thirty-eight years in the Church. For awhile here I was not sure I could stay, since the closing of so many houses means more pressure for space. However, they came across a room which had not been occupied since World War II, so I am in it now.

When I was so uncertain if there was a room available for me...I was serving Mass one Sunday morning, and as I was about to go up to receive Holy Communion, it was as if a voice spoke in the depths of my being this sweet thing: "Why don't you pray for death, Charlie?" There was such an ineffable quality about the sound of these words and they left me with such deep interior peace that I felt they must have been spoken to me from somewhere else than can be imagined or conceived, and which somewhere else we usually describe by the word "heaven," for it did have a heaven-like quality about it, so that it's hard not to believe that it came to me from the place which, due to my age, I soon will be.

Charlie

July 26, 1970

Dear Ronda,

...I have been thinking of dropping you a line for the past few

Letters of Charles Rich / 57

weeks, but the troubles you have make it difficult to know what to say. When it comes to sufferings such as Martin's, the words of the Psalmist come to my mind—"I opened not my mouth because it was thy doing." God lets us suffer without giving us satisfactory reasons for it, because it is His will that, like the Passion of Christ, it should remain a deep mystery, and while it's easy enough to tell ourselves what we have to do, when something like Martin's suffering overtakes our own selves it is a completely different thing. We don't know what graces others have with which to bear the trials of their lot, and so it's useless to make use of words with which to comfort them. Think of Job in this respect, and how his friends were totally unable to comprehend the grief in his heart. And so it is for this reason we all find ourselves so much alone when it comes to bearing the trials of our lot, and only God Himself can at such times be of any sort of consolation to us. Our friends are useless in this respect, because God wants to give us a chance to completely purify us. We would not have this purity if those by whom we are loved could step in between ourselves and God and provide us with their human kind of comfort. Christ alone can do this for us and by means of His own terrible sufferings.

It's important to know this because we would waste so much of our valuable time trying to find relief from our sufferings anywhere else but in Him alone. . . .

Really, Ronda, I don't know what else to say to you, but am anxious to hear from you. My prayer is that Martin should either get his health back or receive the grace from God to bear what he has to in the way which will give him a deeper insight into all things on this earth. This insight can normally only be had by those who suffer a whole lot, and to bear what they have to in a Christ-like manner. Give him my deepest regards and tell him I always have his interests at heart and write soon.

All my love to you both.

Charlie

December 31, 1970

Dear Ronda,

. . . I wish that on this New Year's Eve I could say something to you

58 / The Holy Dybbuk

which would help you love what you now already do even to a more intense degree.... I remember a newly ordained Passionist Father saying to me that he was "hungry for the monastery." I can say the same thing as regards the life I shall soon have in heaven. I can say "I am hungry for heaven" and have been hungry for it since the first day I received the grace to be able to believe in all the wonderful truths of the Catholic religion. But as time passes on and I get to know God better, and gain a deeper insight into those truths, the hunger grows more intense and it gets harder and harder to be resigned to remain away from Christ in His Risen State.

...Strive for the heights, Ronda, since it's only when we are on the heights that the soul is really satisfied and finds life worth living. There is a sublime vista open to the soul, something in the same way as to those who, after heartbreaking labor, reap the reward to look down upon all from the top of Mount Everest. There is a Mount Everest to the truths of our faith to which only the saints alone have the daring and courage to attain—the rest of the faithful being satisfied to view things from a much lower and safer range.

May the year of 1971 be a source of exceptional grace for you, Martin, and the girls.

Charlie

June 29, 1971

Dear Ronda,

I am reading the prophetic portions of Sacred Scripture and as I do so in Hebrew, I am struck by the sheer music of which they are composed. It's like listening the the Fifth Symphony of Beethoven. As you read these sublime poems, you are no longer conscious you are reading Sacred Scripture, but you are lifted up to heights of grandeur and beauty which leave you breathless with thrills and admiration.

How beautiful God's words are in their original forms, and when translated become like wine diluted with water. One of God's great gifts to me is His having given me the grace to read His words as they came from the hands of those who wrote them down....

Charlie

Letters of Charles Rich / 59

December 30, 1972

Hello, dear Ronda,

We both haven't heard from each other for quite a while, so I'm answering your Christmas greeting I just got. May God give you more than can be imagined or conceived and this to you, Martin, and the children.

As for the Pentecostals [*I had written that I had received the charismatic gifts and was part of a prayer group.*—Ed.] I have never been able to let myself be carried away by movements such as these. There have been so many of them throughout the Church's history, and they all evaporated. People sometimes try to make out that St. Francis of Assisi was in his day something like they are today, but they kid themselves. St. Francis loved the hierarchical Church and there was never anyone so thoroughly orthodox. If you want a good analysis of movements like these, read "Enthusiasm" by Ronald Knox. There have been movements like the Pentecostals even among Jewish people at various times in history and they caused them a lot of trouble. It's hard to control such movements, so they invariably get out of hand and end up in all sorts of aberrations.

[*I recall that I was a little miffed by these words of Charlie. I had thought that he would love the spirit of the charismatic renewal with its fervently expressed love for Christ. It seemed to me like a Chasidic Catholicism. Of course I did not want to argue with Charlie about it, but I think that his attitudes about the movement I was so involved in helped to lead to a gradual diminishment of the correspondence after this point. Also, there was a crisis in my life which led me to feel so extremely unholy that I found it embarrassing to read Charlie's letters which always included reference to how holy he thought I was. And so we began to correspond only once or twice a year. Several times I went to New York City and we had lovely meetings together. But it wasn't until 1981 when I received the grace of some pronounced contemplative experiences, that we started up again with an almost daily correspondence. However, I should mention that when Charlie reread this letter in 1984, he told me that he now agreed with me about the positive graces of charismatic prayer.*—Ed.]

Most, or a great deal of my reading now centers itself on the Old

60 / The Holy Dybbuk

Testament in Hebrew. I was especially thrilled when I came across a passage in the book of Job in which God said to Satan "Whence comest thou?" The answer he gave was "walking up and down the earth, to and fro in it." The Hebrew for "walking" has the sense of "to prowl," and by "to and fro" is signified "scourge" and "calamity." It also connotes the idea of "lashing." What wonderful light all this throws on the nature and essence of the evil spirit! How Satan goes about prowling and lashes the soul with all manner of miseries permitted him by God. You can see from this how impoverished translations are and how they deprived the original words from so much strength and meaning and flavor. It's thrilling to make such discoverings and they far outweigh those we make in the external universe, like going to the moon. The real thrills are those we make by delving into the profound mysteries of the Scriptures as we read them in the original tongue. . . .

Well, Ronda, that's all for now. May you and yours be blessed an infinite number of time—and be a great saint.

Charlie

I have no fear of saying you are already, but become an even greater one.

[*As mentioned above, for some seven years we corresponded only infrequently. I was going through many crises, and somehow I was too proud to tell Charlie about them because I didn't want him to have a bad opinion of me. In any case, he was a spiritual friend rather than a director, and so I confided in my director and counselor and left Charlie in some sacrosanct perfect place deep in my soul. After my deep contemplative experiences, when I realized that Charlie was the only person who would understand me from within his own experience, I started writing every day.*

I should also mention that during this time, after many miscarriages, we had a son named Charles, after my husband's father, but the name also had a link in my mind to my spiritual friend, Charles Rich. Also, to my great joy, my husband converted to the Catholic faith after so many years of prayer.—Ed.]

Letters of Charles Rich / 61

January 1, 1982

Dear Ronda,

It's now the third day I am making notes from *The Spiritual Canticle* of St. John of the Cross. I am amazed to see that after reading him over and over for so many years, there are so many insights into his writings that I did not notice till now, and which brings me to the conclusion that if we don't have the time and leisure to read these works over and over in the period of many long years, then there is not much to be derived from them which will be of practical use as far as our relation with God is concerned and the kind of prayer life it is God's will for us to have.

When I first entered the Church forty-eight years ago, I asked my director what he thought of the writings of this Doctor of the Church and if everyone should read them, and here is what he said: "Everyone can read his writings but if one is in serious sin, he should read what will help him along that line, and those who have no time or leisure, they would not be in a position to profit from them." I can now see the truth of these words, since it's over forty-eight years I have read and reread his complete works.

I hope I'm not beginning to bore you with St. John of the Cross, because everything can become dreary if it's over-talked about and over-emphasized.

I don't know what to answer about your question as to why God keeps those who love Him so much and who want to be with Him such a long time in this world. I don't think we'll know the complete answer to this question till we get to heaven, for like so many other things connected with our love for Christ, they are meant to remain a deep mystery, a mystery of love and faith.

Last night, while lying in bed trying to get to sleep, it seemed as if heaven opened up and I could see all that's there waiting for me. The intense joy of heart this experience produced in my soul was so overwhelming, that I felt if it lasted more than a few minutes more than it did, I'd die of the sheer delight and joy of it. I don't remember anything like it. I have certainly received many favors from God, but this experience transcended them all. Is it possible God wanted to give

62 / The Holy Dybbuk

me a taste of the joys of heaven into which, as the result of my age, He sees I shall soon enter?

That's all, Ronda dear, and may God bless you an infinite number of times and reward you for loving Him so much, with everything you have from Him.

Charlie

January 3, 1982

Dear Ronda,

...I can't see any good reason for resorting to unusual means of prolonging my life, since, according to my directors, I am not morally obliged to do so.

I always call to mind the words of St. Robert Bellarmine in which he says, "I want to go to my home; I have lived long enough." Every time the new year came around he said, "Am I never going to die?" That's how anxiously as a saint, he wanted to get out of this world so as to be in that way completely with Christ. Can we be completely with Him in any other way than by getting out of this world?

Reason alone tells me to have lived to the age I am in (82) is to have lived long enough, and so I should not be in a hurry to rush for medical treatment. [*I believe this concerned a small patch of skin under his eye which could be cancerous—later on references to ill health will refer also to a prostate condition deemed cancerous by a doctor.*—Ed.]

St. Thomas More, I think it was, who said that if we are in every sickness to ask to be cured, when will we be ready to die? It's absurd and ridiculous to ask God to be cured in every sickness we are in, since we will in that way never dispose ourselves for going home to heaven and to enjoy Him there instead of the mere "sips" of Him we get on this earth, or the "crumbs" St. John of the Cross speaks about.

There is a beautiful passage from St. Jane of Chantal: "What are we doing in this life, my dear sisters? I can assure you that I never had so clear a view of the goodness and beauty of death."

...From the last two or so letters, I have the feeling that you are growing up in Christ and you have now reached adulthood in Him, so that's a source of delight to know.

Letters of Charles Rich / 63

... Well, Ronda, grow up in Christ, for if you do you won't distress yourself by anything at all that God either wills or allows to take place in this life. With Him it's eternity alone that matters and not this puny existence. Think of eternity and let your heart and mind dwell in the place of delight that holy word stands for and in which same, as a daughter of Mary, you will so be and so will I with you.

God-by [*sic*] in our divine Lord who has done so much for the both of us and who has been so sweetly and so marvelously good to us in giving us to each other in a mystical and divine and heavenly sweet way. So love in Him and in Him alone.

Charlie

Don't force yourself to write long letters if it conflicts with your work in class.

April 15, 1982

Dear Ronda,

... Last night this thought came to me: I was going to ask that you get me into heaven by your prayer so that when I get there I will pray that you should get there too. But after due consideration, I felt it better to leave such things in God's hands, since He knows best how to dispose things for our eternal well-being.

I don't thing it's possible to have more joy than the kind I experience when I read about the love for Christ with which your heart and mind is now blessedly filled. I love you very much, Ronda, in Him who is Love Itself, and not outside of Him, since love outside and apart from the Love Itself Christ is, is not worth the affection of our hearts. You are growing more dear to the Heart of Christ with each letter I get from you. ...

Charlie

June 10, 1982

Dear Ronda,

Your letters to me are full of so many deep thoughts and even more beautiful feelings, that it would take pages on pages to comment

64 / *The Holy Dybbuk*

worthily on them and tell you how much I appreciate your writing them and love to read them.

As to the question as to whether it is you or I who have changed, the answer is most definite that you have changed. You have really not changed, only the treasures of soul in you have been sort of bottled-up, so they are now uncorked.

I remember reading that it takes two to tell the truth: one to speak and the other to listen, and I think it's along this line we can get an idea of the importance the doctrine of the Mystical Body of Christ is, and of the words "where two or three are gathered together in my name, there I am in the midst of you," because, in a spiritual way, one human being needs another in order to develop and grow.

During the first fourteen years of my entry into the Church, I went to the same director and I now realize that without his help, love, and encouragement, I would never have been able to live the sort of life it has been God's will for me.

We need each other in this world and we will need each other to share in the joys of the life to come, and, as there is a Mystical Body on earth, there will be one in heaven for all eternity. We shall be with each other there, Ronda, and it's this conviction which is the basis of earthly friendships in Christ.

It is said that a friendship that has an end was never true friendship. If this is true in the natural order, how much more true is it in the supernatural state in which we now are and in which we shall continue to be for all eternity. And it's too bad there are not more friendships in Christ, the kind had by all the saints. Can the relationship between two human beings be more intimate and more holy than was the one between St. Jane Chantal and her great spiritual director, St. Francis de Sales? Were it not for his friendship for her, there would have been a saint less in the Church of God. . . .

Charlie

July 3, 1982

Dear Ronda,

Have you read much, if any, of the writings of the Venerable Francis

Letters of Charles Rich / 65

Libermann, the only Jewish convert who has been declared Venerable since the Holy Office was founded some four hundred years ago? I came across some of his words in a letter he wrote and they go like this: "I do not wish you to pass through the painful ordeal through which I have passed. God grant that life may not be such a burden as it has been to me! I can hardly pass over a bridge without being assailed by the thought of throwing myself into the river, to put an end to my sufferings. But Jesus sustains me and gives me patience."

It's sometimes good to read words like these, for they help us realize that the way to heaven is strewn with miseries of every conceivable kind. So much so is this the case that we sometimes wonder why people want to become saints, seeing there is such a vast amount of suffering to go through in the process of becoming one. You have yourself had a goodly share of such sufferings, and it's these which are responsible for you now being so close to the Heart of Christ, and you'll get even closer to that Heart as time passes and you make progress along the road of sanctity.

I say this to you to encourage you to strive for the heights of bliss that knowing and loving Christ in a deep intimate way involves, and from which way many, who are otherwise good Catholics, shrink. You'll be in heaven one day, but before you'll have the happiness of getting there, much ground will have to be covered along the way of the Cross. Christ went ahead of us along that way, so it's now possible, with the help of God's grace, to follow in the footsteps of all the saints.

. . .

Charlie

July 7, 1982

Dear Ronda,

The closer we draw to God and the older we grow, the more God allows aridity in prayer to increase.

It's now around 2:00 A.M. so on account of the aridity, I don't know what to do with myself along spiritual and prayer lines. I am too weak to read, and if I go down to the chapel, I fall asleep.

Now when I said that the reason I wrote you one of the letters was

66 / *The Holy Dybbuk*

because I did not know what to do with myself, I really paid you a compliment, because writing that letter to you really put me back into the state of prayer. It did this because I talked about God in that letter, so I was really and actually praying.

You write poems when you pray, so it's for this reason you rightfully call them prayer-poems. I also pray when I write to you, so the letters should really be called prayer-letters. In short, writing to you places my soul in a state of prayer, so it's for this reason I enjoy writing you. . . .

Charlie

August 5, 1982

Dear Ronda,

It seems the years are catching up with me, especially the eyes. But when I think the whole thing over I say to myself, "how can I complain about my eyes seeing they have served me so faithfully for eighty-two years?" The same is true as to the rest of the bodily faculties.

. . . Years ago, when I did not think, or had doubts, whether it's God's will I should write down my meditations, my director told me that whatever gifts I had along that line were meant to be shared with others and that we just don't hug all the graces God gives us all by ourselves.

One reason for asking this question was due to the fact that my entire formal schooling consisted of three years of grade school. I arrived in this country at the age of ten. After spending three years in public school, my Father got me to take out my working papers at the age of thirteen. From that day on I never went to school. With such a background I felt there was considerable doubt for me to presume to want to put my thoughts into writing.

Nevertheless, I followed my director's advice though I was kind of reluctant. That was about forty years ago.

Years ago I met a priest who intimated that the views I hold may not be according to God along doctrinal lines. So the next time I saw my director I mentioned what the priest said to me. When I did this, I noticed the expression of my director's face change, and in a stern and resolute voice he said these words to me: "Be forthright." He said this

Letters of Charles Rich / 67

because he detected a certain misgiving on my part at the direct way I have of expressing myself.

Charlie

August 9, 1982

Dear Ronda,

...How profoundly Catholic all the saints are and with what devotion they served the hierarchical Church! There was never a saint who, in the words of St. Paul, did not "think with the mind of Christ," and what a contrast this is to some of our liberal theologians who go out of their way to deviate from the Church's teachings and who, in this way, murder souls. I think God can forgive any sin, except the sin of undermining one's faith in the teachings of the Church. ...

Charlie

August 12, 1982

Dear Ronda,

...The best thing about your letter of this morning is the sentence: "Oh dear Charlie, we are saints and we are going to heaven because He loves us so dearly, yes, yes, yes."

It's years now I have been hoping for you to say such words. That's why reading them delights me so much. I am always delighted when I see people having the courage and daring to love God the way all the saints have done, since such love entails deep faith in the goodness of God's putting up with our shortcomings, and pouring His gifts into us in spite of these shortcomings, as St. Gregory observes. ...

Charlie

August 13, 1982

Dear Ronda,

...Why don't more good Catholics go all the way? Why are so many of them satisfied with the word "good" when it's God's will they should only be satisfied with the word "saint"? I guess it's too much to

68 / *The Holy Dybbuk*

want to know in this life why this is so, and why more good people don't want to be all that the patriarchs and the prophets of the Old Testament have been, and with the saints and the Apostles of the New, as well as all the saints who have lived since then.

...St Elizabeth Seton wrote a letter to the man who was directly responsible for her conversion to the Catholic faith, and these are the words: "You have led me to a happiness which admits of no description!" In another letter to him she said, "Oh, for the language of heaven where everything will be made known by a look of the soul."

These are beautiful words, so I often like to call them to mind. Where would we be today without the saints? Would this world not be a dreary place in which to live without a St. Francis of Assisi, a St. Francis de Sales, a St. Bernard, a St. John of the Cross, a St. Teresa, and the innumerable others it would be too wearying to mention by name. Has not Leon Bloy said that the only tragedy is not to have become a saint?

It is, Ronda, so I am glad to hear that you have finally made up your mind to walk along the paths trodden by the Saint of Saints, and all the others after Him. There is a beautiful passage in the book of Isaiah that has always fascinated me. It reads: "A highway will be there, called the holy way; No one unclean may pass over it, nor fools go astray on it. No lion will be there, nor beast of prey go up to be met upon it. . . . and on it the redeemed will walk" (Is. 35:8-9).

Do not these words have reference to the path of holiness on which all the saints have walked and on which you now have the grace to accompany them?

Charlie

[*Loose sheets without dates from around this period.*—Ed.]

...St. Gertrude tells us that she had such deep and intimate experiences of Christ, experiences of love for Him, that she was afraid of expressing those experiences, because reading of them would scandalize those who did not have such experiences. In her Revelations she says that our Lord appeared to her as a "youth of sixteen years and of

Letters of Charles Rich / 69

ravishing beauty." I have always loved her for not being afraid to speak of having seen Christ as a youth of sixteen and of indescribable beauty.

. . . If ever the devil wills to perform a great masterpiece of diabolism, it is to try to convince people that God does not love them and that their aspirations for deep spirituality and high holiness are illusory.

I once said to a priest I went to confession to that I wanted to be a martyr, and he flushed with anger and gave me a good calling down. I only went to this priest a few times. But I once asked my great spiritual director whom I had for fourteen years and who, when he died, was called a saint by his fellow Jesuits (Fr. Clark), if I could take the vow taken by St. John Brebeuf. This vow specifies that if there is a chance to avoid giving your life in defense of your faith, you should not be allowed to do so. Fr. Clark said that there is little likelihood of having to face such persecution in this country, but he nevertheless gave me permission to take the vow. . . .

Fr. Clark was one of the greatest human beings I have so far met in this life, and the kind of spirituality he recommended was the one practiced by all the saints. I have always felt since the very first day of my baptism, that for me to be a saint is the same thing as to be a Catholic and that, if I failed to strive for sanctity, there was no point in my practicing my Catholic faith. I have always equated Catholicism with sanctity, for to me they were always one.

Charlie

August 23, 1982

Dear Ronda,

. . . in spite of all the infirmities one at my age incurs in a physical way, I never had such deep peace and I would not exchange the happiness I experience by loving God, the way He graciously permits me to, with all the pleasures this world has to offer. It's astounding how close to heaven we can get and the indescribable joys we can experience right here on this earth. Along this line, does not St. Augustine say to us these words: "the angels alone are truly rich."

70 / *The Holy Dybbuk*

. . . Years before I became a Catholic, I used to entertain myself with the thought that when I die I will meet the authors of the great masterpieces of literature like Shakespeare, Dante, and others like them. I thought what a wonderful thing it will be to meet them in the next life. Since my conversion, I now think what a great thing it will be to meet all the saints I have learned to love so much and whose writings I have read over and over and which same have become a part of my own way of looking at things. What a grace it will be to meet a St. Teresa in the next life and a St. John of the Cross and a St. Bernard. The list is endless.

Do you have any thoughts like these every once in awhile, and aren't they consoling beyond measure?

Charlie

August 25, 1982

Hello Ronda,

I spent the last two days reading Spenser and I am now tackling Robert Browning's poetry, which I have already read many times. I remember years back when I got kind of scrupulous reading poetry and asked my holy and learned director about the matter and here is what he said: "The psalms are poetry."

I think there is a connection between poetry and religion and that the former, like any work of art and beauty, can serve as a step to the Supreme Beauty that God is.

As far as Browning is concerned, he is not easy reading, but he is deeply spiritual and a poet of the first rank with some beautiful lines. Here are a few:

"And I shall behold thee, face to face,
O God, and in thy light retrace
How in all I loved here, still wast thou!"

The next line is from his great masterpiece *The Ring*, the book which someone said "is the most profound spiritual treasure that England has produced since the days of Shakespeare." This is an enormous work and requires great patience on account of its originality. Here are a couple of lines from it:

Letters of Charles Rich / 71

[...]"through such souls alone,
God stooping shows sufficient of His light
for us in the dark to rise by. And I rise."
I better stop with these two quotes because there are so many
beautiful lines in him that one could never stop quoting them.

Charlie

August 1982

Dear Ronda,
I am very intrigued by what you say about the Holy Dybbuk taking
up his abode in your heart after I die and find no place on earth for
myself. You, of course, realize that the whole dybbuk idea is only
fanciful imagination and that there is no basis for it in fact and that it is
not theologically true.

Still, like all legends and fanciful imaginations, there is a grain of
truth in this idea, because, as I have already so often said to you,
everything that's waiting for us in the next life has its beginning on
earth, like the Psalmist tells us when he says, "Taste and see that the
Lord is sweet." David is here referring to the taste on earth of what the
joys of heaven are like, so along this line, why cannot we have a taste
on earth and an experience of what our relationship will be in the next
life—at least a tiny taste and experience of that relationship. We have
this taste and experience in the spiritual feeling of now being with
each other in some wonderfully and indescribable way, along the
dybbuk idea.

I fully believe that there can be a relationship in Christ between two
human beings of so pure and so sublime and so mystical a nature that it
will in some way resemble the relationship we shall have with each
other in the next life. . . . Are we not told that we shall, after this life is
over, be as the holy angels are and that we will then share in their own
prerogatives. Now if this is Scripturally true, coming to us from the
mouth of Christ Himself, why cannot we now in this life get a slight
experience of our angelic state after we die?

. . . It is such a rare and extraordinary kind that it can only exist
between two people who have given themselves up completely to love
for Christ and who, in everything they do, seek only God's greater

72 / The Holy Dybbuk

glory. It exists between those whose love for Christ is the same as was the love for Christ had by all the saints. . . . Is it not the teaching of the Mystical Body of Christ that we are now in this life mystically one with our divine Lord, and if we are mystically one with Christ on earth, won't we be mystically one with Him in the life to come, and in this oneship, are not those we have the grace to now love in Christ, included in this kind of relationship?

All I am trying to say in these tortuous words is that I now look at you in the same way as I will have the grace to do when we are both in heaven. I do this, of course, in a very limited degree, the degree to which it is possible under the conditions of this life.

It is said of a saint that every time he saw a woman, he saw the Blessed Virgin in that woman. It was a mystical kind of perception he had the grace to have. . . . Besides, aren't we told to see Christ Himself in one another, and it's this I am trying to do in reference not only to your own dear self but to everyone else with whom I come into intimate contact.

Well, Ronda, I guess I better stop before spoiling what I already said. St. John of the Cross said that there were certain extraordinary experiences of God about which he did not want to say more than he had already done, for fear that one might get the idea, the wrong idea, that there was not more to be said of that kind of experience. . . .

Pray for me, Ronda, because I hold you very dear in the Heart we both have the grace to be held in.

Charlie

August 1982

Dear Ronda,

The problems you have in your home life are normal ones and your reactions to them are the kind you should have towards them. I'd be suspicious of your advanced prayer life if you did not feel the way you do as regards all things concerning your home life. We are not in paradise and it's only when we will be there that everything will be to our heart's content.

I think I remember saying to you what my second great Jesuit

Letters of Charles Rich / 73

director said to me when I gave him a review of all the troubles I had. He said, "the only solution to the problem of life is embalming fluid." And I have since then accepted this solution to be God's will for me.

Then you have the words of St. Paul when he says he would rather depart and be with Christ, but he is willing to stay here in this life if it's necessary for the well-being of others that he be away from the place of his heart's desire.

As I have told you, I have for years prayed for death, but stopped doing so—praying for God's will for me instead.

We'll only be what we want to be when we get to heaven and this is true as regards our spiritual life, since it's only there we shall be able to love God the way He wishes we should love Him. In this respect, St. Francis de Sales says we are all "novices" and that "the perfect conjunction of the soul with God will only take place in the next life."

Here, in this life, we have to struggle and strive for what we will attain in the one to come, so with this in view don't let it surprise you that things are what they are and that the problems you have in your home life are what you say they are. It's in heaven that there are ideal wives, ideal husbands, ideal children, and everything else we can think of on this earth.

... I can't help calling to mind the words of St. Robert Bellarmine, SJ, who, as he approached the end of his valuable and fruitful life as a saint and scholar, used to say these words to those about him who kept telling him of the need the Church had for his wisdom and guidance: "I want to go to my house," he kept on saying, calling heaven his home. "I have lived long enough." Now being what he was, a holy and learned person, he can't be charged with misdirected zeal. Everyone who genuinely loves God wants to be with Him in His high heaven. ... I am also, at the same time, ready to stay in this life another thousand years if God so wills and that is what counts since "in His will is our peace," Dante says in his Divine Comedy. ...

Charlie

August 31, 1982

Dear Ronda,

When St. Bernardine was dying, these were the words he kept

74 / *The Holy Dybbuk*

saying: "Love, Love, Love, see to it that there always be love in your hearts."

St. Augustine tells us that the only commandment that was given was the one to love. In the commentary I wrote on the Song of Songs, I said that there can never be enough of love.

. . . Outside of Christ nothing is worth having, because outside of Christ nothing persists, and if it does not persist, of what good is it?
. . .

Charlie

September 7, 1982

Dear Ronda,

Late this afternoon, after a friend left, I went to the Students' Chapel with the intention of spending some time in it. After being there a while, a feeling of lonesomeness came over me. I felt the need for the kind of companionship that cannot be had in the present life. God, I felt, was far off, and the kind of companionship to be had from a human being is inadequate to satisfy the soul's needs. Does it not say in the psalms: "I shall be satisfied when I shall appear in Thy presence," or, "when thy glory shall appear."

Realizing all this, that human companionship cannot now give us what we will receive from it in the next life, and that we cannot now have God in the way the soul needs to have Him, in all His fullness, this realization produces a deep loneliness in the soul's depth. So much can be said along this line, but there are in this life no words to do it with.

I said I will not send any more quotes, but perhaps I was too hasty in saying this. There are a few quotes from St. Catherine of Genoa and Blessed Angela of Foligno, that I can't resist sending you—that is if you have not already read them yourself.

Here is the one from St. Catherine: "If a man were to take a soul from Paradise, how do you think such a soul would feel? You might give it all the pleasures in the world, and as much more as you can imagine: and yet, all would be but Hell, because of the memory of the divine union formerly possessed and now lost."

The other is from Blessed Angela: "Then did my soul feel an assurance so true that it doubted no more. It had such joy that neither man nor saint come down from heaven could declare it. Then He told me that He concealed much love, because I was not able to bear it; my soul answered: 'If you are God, omnipotent, make me able to bear it.' Then He made answer finally and said: 'If I were to do as you ask, you would have here all that you desire and would no longer hunger after Me. For this reason I will not grant your request, for I desire in this world you should hunger and long for me and should be eager to find Me.' "

...There is something Goethe said that has always affected me deeply: "Human nature possesses wonderful powers and has some good things in readiness for us when we least hope for it. There have been times when I have fallen asleep in tears, but in my dreams the most charming forms have come to console and cheer me, and I have arisen the next morning fresh and joyful." I have always been grateful to Goethe for these words and feel he must have saved his soul in the Catholic sense as the result of them. ...

Charlie

September 8, 1982

Dear Ronda,

...It's 2 A.M. and I am in the house chapel with the assurance that there will be no one in it for another three hours, making prayer delightful to practice.

Whenever I am here in this chapel the early part of the morning, the thought of you is very vivid to my mind and so I spend some time in it praying for the sanctification of your immortal soul. In a mystical way I feel you are close by....

What a wonderful thing love for Christ is and how love for Him invigorates and refreshes the soul. ...

When I think I shall soon be with the holy angels and the faithful departed, my soul leaps with joy. This joy becomes so intense I think I can't go on living in a life in which we cannot have God in all fullness.
...

Charlie

76 / *The Holy Dybbuk*

September 9, 1982

Dear Ronda,

...Goethe, though not of our own faith, says: "Man should believe in immortality; he has a right to this belief; it corresponds with the wants of his nature and he may believe in the promises of religion. ...To me the eternal existence of the soul is proved from my idea of activity; if I work on incessantly till my death, nature is bound to give me another form of existence when the present one can no longer sustain my spirit." ...from his translator Bayard Taylor: "And over all broods the Germanic spirit, ever ready in the midst of time to cast a longing gaze upon eternity."

Also, all this corresponds with what my first director told me when I asked him to give me some sort of criteria where I should and should not be, and he said: "Wherever you find yourself and do not hear the word "eternity" mentioned frequently, that is no place for you to be." You have heard these words before from me, but they are worth repeating. ...

I look forward to December, and as regards my staying in this life till you get here, that's of course in God's hands, but there is no concern about such matters, since if I go to heaven before you get here, I'll be closer to you than I could be physically and be of even greater assistance to you spiritually than you say I now am.

Love Charles

September 10, 1982

Dear Ronda,

...Can we be too wild in our love for Him who lowered Himself to the degree that He did! When it comes to mystical prayer, it's so easy to mistake the ungenuine for the genuine one. They say that Ignatius Loyola said that for every true mystic there are ninety-nine false ones, and even one hundred. I don't know if he really said this, but it's certainly an exaggeration, because Scaramelli, SJ, who did missionary work for thirty years, has written a very masterly treatise on mysticism. When he was asked why, after spending his life doing missionary work he wrote this treatise, he said that during these thirty years he came across all sorts of people who, in his eyes, had received genuine

Letters of Charles Rich / 77

mystical graces, so he felt the need for writing on that subject. . . . I say this because I have not yet detected one false note in your mystical experiences of God and so this makes me very happy and I thank God for His goodness to you along that line.

The reason your prayer life is so sound is due to the fact that you have been on the cross and that God will continue to keep you on it, since that's the only way we can be protected from illusions and delusions in our prayer life and in our mystical relationship with our divine Lord. . . . as I told you, in a quote by Frederick Ozanam, whose Cause has been introduced, "Ordinary Catholics are plentiful enough; we need saints." . . .

I just got back from seeing Tom and so I feel kind of worn out. His health does not improve with time, but is getting steadily worse. Spiritually, though, he is as alert as ever as far as the things of God are concerned. I have already mentioned to you the fact that every time I go to see him I come back spiritually refreshed. Someone more thoroughly reconciled to the acceptance of God's will in suffering, I don't know. If he was a member of a religious community, he'd be canonized. Living all alone by himself, there are no others to carry out the necessary steps that have to do with being raised up to the altars of the Church.

. . . I am so worn out that I am too tired to go down to the Chapel, but I feel God understands and so there is no cause for concern.

I know of no one who loves to spend time in Church more than Tom, and yet due to his condition he is unable to satisfy his desire along this line. He does all his praying in his home, and it's probably more heartfelt than anyone who lives in a cloistered community. Tom is very strong in this respect of having to be satisfied to do all his praying by himself and away from the Blessed Sacrament. He only now and then can get to Church.

I admire him in this respect because I have to have the help of being in Chapel to feel intimately united to Our Lord. In short, Tom's faith is even stronger than mine, because it's strong enough not to need being in Church. It takes strong faith to be united to God no matter where one may find himself and under the most diverse circumstances which are not favorable to a life of recollection in God. . . .

Charlie

78 / *The Holy Dybbuk*

September 17, 1982

Dear Ronda,

...I don't feel much like writing today because interiorly I am kind of dry. The problem, the great one, is that the closer one draws to God by the graces of prayer he gets, and especially contemplative and mystical prayer, the more that person will have to experience large periods of aridity and spiritual dryness. This does not occur at the beginning of such a life, because if it did, no one would have the courage even to set out on such a journey, the one mystical and contemplative prayer is, and which same prayer you have the grace to have.

...Mystical writers all go out of their way to warn those whom God is raising to mystical union with Himself about the periods in their lives in which they would feel they did not even have the same faith ordinary Catholics possess, since they don't get any kind of consolations from the practice of their faith. It's the purgatorial state in the lives of contemplatives, and which same none of even the greatest saints were exempted. At such times the thought of one's own death is the only consolation there is and that nothing lasts in this world, including the trials of the mystical life.

...St. Philip Neri used to say that we should only read books by an author whose name begins with an "S" (Saint), and I have faithfully, with rare exceptions, followed that advice.

There are too many masterpieces of mystical writing by the saints of the Church to go to non-Catholic authors on that subject. Maybe I am a little too narrow along that line. But mysticism being such a delicate subject, we can't be too cautious in reading books on it, so the best protection is to go to the saints for security and safety....

About two weeks ago, I was on the steps leading to the ground floor, when all of a sudden I felt my inner being light up in a way I would not attempt to describe. It was as if I was suddenly transported into another world, the one eternity is.

The whole thing lasted only a few seconds, and after it was over, I tried to note down what I just felt. It was a feeling of delight so excessive that I no longer felt myself to be where I was. It was as if heaven opened up and I got a glimpse of what was there. The only

Letters of Charles Rich / 79

thing I remember about that experience is a kind of delight too overwhelming to even try to express. It was as if I saw God Himself. I don't know if I should have told you this, but the effect of that experience has never left me, so I feel I should share the joy it brought to my inner being, illuminating that inner being in a way too marvelously sweet for any kind of expression....

... As for music, I do love it, because does not St. Paul say: "Whatever is good, whatever is lovely, etc., think of these things," and in which same music, poetry, painting, sculpture, and all the great literary masterpieces are included, since there is nothing God made and inspires others to make, which cannot be a means to Himself, if made use of with that intention in view, namely, His greater glory.

So, with this in view, I have a cassette on which I play Bach's *St. Matthew Passion.* I also have tapes of *La Boheme, Tosca, Turandot, La Traviata, Rigoletto,* and *Aida.* And this means I am making use of God's creatures as a step to Himself, though at times when I feel myself close to God, all these things don't do me any good, and I could not listen to them if I tried, there being times for creature satisfactions and others when only the uncreated good things of God can afford any help to the soul, and primarily, the Creator alone of all these good, true, and beautiful things of which St. Paul speaks and of which he counsels us to make use for the glory of God.

I am delighted to hear you got Poulain [*The Graces of Interior Prayer*]. It's been my favorite book on mystical prayer even before I was a Catholic—that's over fifty years ago. I have since, and during all these years, read and reread every single page of this book, which Fr. Clark told me is "the best book on prayer there is." If more people who are gifted with the gifts of prayer read this book, there would be less false prayer along the higher stages of the spiritual and mystical life.

On page 404 you will find these important words which, if more people gifted with mystical graces would make their own, there would be less false mysticism in the world. Here is the passage: "The expression 'sensible consolation' and its synonyms 'sensible devotion,' 'sensible tastes,' do not signify a consolation that is felt, for all consolation is more or less felt. It refers to consolation of the lower order, that which has its beginning in the sense or sensible faculties. We must not

80 / The Holy Dybbuk

despise it on this account, because it leads us finally to good.

"When the saints lifted up their hearts to God by contemplating the beauties of nature, this was sensible devotion. The Church also makes use of sensible means when she captivates our ears with her chants, or our eyes with noble architecture, pictures, statues, or the pomp of her ceremonial. Protestantism was wrong in rejecting nearly all of these aids, wishing to address itself to man's highest faculties only. His whole nature should be appealed to.

"St. John of the Cross is not speaking to all Christians indiscriminately when he counsels the rejection of sensible consolations. He is only concerned with those who are beginning to enjoy the mystic state, and he simply asks them to give it the preference when it encounters any obstacle in devotions of the sensible order and the pleasure felt in them. When no such conflict occurs, we must resort to all the means that can lead us towards God."

...I am also happy to hear my letters don't distract you from the duties of your family life. If they did, I would not write you another word, because your whole prayer life would then be false and illusory. Poulain speaks of those who give themselves over falsely to a life of prayer and this at the expense of the duties of their state. With you, though, the case is the exact opposite, so it is for this reason I feel so consoled to read your letters on account of the soundness of your prayer life. ...

Charlie

P.S.   At the bottom of page 405 [Poulain] there is this note of St. Alphonsus Liguori: "Spiritual consolations are gifts which are much more precious than all the riches and honors of this world. And if the sensibility itself is aroused, that completes our devotion, for then the whole being is united to God and tastes God. That sensibility is to be dreaded when it takes us away from God, but it is very well ordered when it unites us to God. (Love for Jesus Christ, ch. xvii. See also Suarez, *De Orat.* Book II, ch. xviii, a, i.4.)

Along this line, there is a passage in *The Ascent of Mt. Carmel* which is rarely quoted: "I should like to offer a norm for discovering when this gratification of the senses is beneficial and when it is not. Whenever a person, upon hearing music or other things, seeing agreeable objects, smelling sweet fragrance, or feeling the delight of

Letters of Charles Rich / *81*

certain tastes and delicate touches immediately at the first moment directs his thoughts and the affections of his will to God, receiving more satisfaction in the thought of God than in the sensible object that caused it, and finds no gratification in the senses save for this motive, it is a sign that he is profiting by the senses and that the sensory part is a help to the spirit. The senses can then be used because the sensorial objects serve the purpose for which God created them: that He be more known and loved (page 255 Mt. Carmel Edition).

September 25, 1982

Dear Ronda,

...as we go on progressing in our prayer life, the consolations we get are more interior and more substantial. As St. John of the Cross puts it, "It's a touch of the substance of God in the substance of the soul." ...

There have to be sufferings with the graces God gives us, and the greater and more abundant these graces, the greater the suffering that accompany them. I once spoke to a Jesuit about prayer and this is what he said to me: "I'd be afraid to pray because I would have to suffer." Are not these revealing words? Another priest whom I met over forty years ago, and who has since then become a saint, said these words to me at that time: "I am afraid of suffering."

Good Catholics are very foolish in their being afraid of the Cross, because with the Cross comes a sweetness from heaven so intense and overwhelming that had God in His goodness not moderated that sweetness from heaven, the soul would be forced from the body, that sweetness forcing the soul to leave the body.

The main thing with being a saint is remaining one, since we read of St. John seeing the stars fall from heaven, and these stars are those who were called to high holiness but who failed to persevere in their holy state.

I have once written you the words of one saint to another in which this saint said: "You are a saint, but remain what you are." The only problem you will ever have is to remain being as close to God as you now have the grace to be, and this on account of the sufferings, moral

82 / The Holy Dybbuk

ones, you will have to go through and of which suffering you speak in your letter this morning, the suffering caused you by seeing those you know not loving the Love God is in the way you have the grace to do. . . .

There is a great truth in your saying "we need a daily model of the holy life, and this is something different from seeing a director from time to time." In my case this was the same person, because the director I had for the first fourteen years in the Church was acknowledged by all as not only one of the greatest of all directors, but also a saint. When he died those who knew him had no doubt along this line. [*This is the often-mentioned Fr. Clark, S.J.*—Ed.]

Without having had a director who was also a saint, there is no doubt in my mind I would not have been able to live the way I did all these years. It was seeing him so close to God that gave me the grace to follow the advice he gave me. Many times I had such a holy awe for both his wisdom and his holiness that I was tempted to kneel in adoration of him. He is the greatest human being I so far have met on this earth and any help I can give you along lines of prayer is due to his helping me along the same lines. I merely pass on to you what I have received from him.

Love in Christ,

Charlie

October 1, 1982

Dear Ronda,

Quotes are good and beautiful to have and read and I'll keep sending them to you without number, but it's still more important to relive in our own lives the truths and beauties of them. . . .

Many good people have a false kind of humility. . .because God, being infinitely rich, wants us to expect great things from Him, and St. Teresa speaks somewhere of a king paying a visit to a poor peasant and asking that poor person what he would have from him, and this poor person just asks for a single penny. The moral is so clear it needs no comment.

St. Bernard tells us that "Moses was not afraid to ask great things

Letters of Charles Rich / 83

from God, because he was himself great," and don't we read God saying "open wide thy mouth that I may fill it," and which words mean we should have great and immortal longings in ourselves and not worry too much about being presumptuous along this line, because it's a presumption dear to the heart of Christ. It's only when we love someone very much we are not afraid to ask great things from him, knowing the love we have for that person will serve to explain our presumption. . . .

Isaiah asks this question: "Has God's hand been shortened?" It has not, and this because there are now, at this terrible and awful ungodly age, saints as great as any in the past. But being alive, and to protect their humility, God does not make this known to them. There are still St. Gertrudes in the world and St. Catherines and St. Teresas, etc.

I have for many years had this idea: There are many things in this life not everyone can be. Everyone cannot become a doctor of medicine, an attorney at law, a college professor, or an artist. But everyone can become a saint, and what are all these professions, compared to the profession of becoming a saint? Nothing at all, Ronda, since there can be no proportion between the two types of careers. Everyone, no matter what state he may be in, can, if he so wills, become as great a saint as anyone who has ever lived, and to say he cannot is to deny God's ability to make him one, and which same denial is nothing short of being heretical.

. . . I cannot close without one more quote from Heinrich Suso: "Put up with your inferior nature inherited from Adam, as willingly as with the higher you share in Christ."

Charlie

No date

Dear Ronda,

. . . As to your two letters of this morning, it was distressing to read of the kind of stuff they now teach, so I refuse to read that kind of garbage. There is nothing so banal and unoriginal as falsehood and

84 / *The Holy Dybbuk*

error, and downright heresy is as old as the world and it has been promulgated since the early days of both Judaism and Christianity. There have always been those who have denied the basic truths of faith, and that kind of denial will go on existing till the end of time. I feel very sorry for all such denyers because they must be miserable at heart to do such denial, so I pray for them.

As for you, you have to follow your director's advice in this matter, so I can make no comment. [*This problem concerned a priest who had denied the existence of the angels at a sermon on the Feast of St. Michael and St. Gabriel.*—Ed.] My job is to help you pray and love the truths of the holy Catholic Faith, for which same millions have given their lives. It will be quite a thing for those who now deny the basic truths of the Christian religion to face those who died for those truths in the next life.

Anyway, I was so distressed by what I read that I tore up the letters. God does not want me to get involved in public disputes, but to suffer, pray, and make atonement for sin in the trials I am allowed to go through. So, in future letters keep out the falsehoods that seem so prevalent today. At least, in my case, it's often a virtue to bury my head in the sand, because in order to live the kind of life it's God's will for me to live, I must keep my soul at peace and let others with different vocations carry on their combats for the truth. Besides, I am too close to eternal rest to carry on such warfare—the warfare I carry on is the kind St. Paul speaks about in the seventh chapter of his Epistle to the Romans....

Charlie

October 7, 1982

Dear Ronda,

...There are still many things in me that require that kind of purification, since as St. John of the Cross says, if we don't want to undergo the purifying effects of purgatory after this life is over, then we must be willing to accept the trials of this life in place of the purgatorial experiences we will have to undergo in the life to come. Does not Job say that the "angels are not pure in His sight"?

Letters of Charles Rich / 85

Still, all this does not really matter, since it's really the mercy of God that will get us to heaven, and there is nothing we can do on our part that can entitle us to the kind of happiness we will there experience. . . .

Charlie

October 8, 1982

Dear Ronda,

. . . Yesterday, on my way to see some friends on Long Island, I got deathly sick when I boarded the train, and so, following my instincts, I left it a few minutes before the train left Penn Station.

I am not going to go into the details of this sickness, but for a whole day and night afterwards I felt drained and weak. So this made me realize that while it's all right to pray when we are well physically, when we are ill along that line, the prayer takes the form of being resigned to God's will in that sickness.

It also made me realize that when we get sick, we get more detached from all the world has to offer in one hour than we would become by hours, and even months, when we have nothing bitter to bear. It's then we feel that the test is if we really love God—when God takes away from us all His consolations.

I think sickness that drains us mentally and physically gives us a taste of death, the feebleness we feel then making us fit for nothing at all. . . .

Charlie

October 9, 1982

Dear Ronda,

. . . This morning in chapel, I felt very arid and could get no consolation from praying. St. Augustine says that if we practiced the three virtues of faith, hope, and charity to a heroic degree, we would not even need the Scriptures except for the purpose of teaching others. Blessed Angela of Foligno said that when she was in the state of prayer, everything that's written about Christ in the Scriptures was "only a

86 / *The Holy Dybbuk*

hindrance." This morning I felt the truth of her words, since I could get no consolation from anything I ever read.

To detach us even from supernatural things, God allows us not to derive any consolation from even the most sublime things we read in the writings of the saints. St. John Chrysostom says that before sin was committed, there was no need for written words, since God's laws were engraved in the heart that made the written words we now have in the Scriptures unnecessary.

. . . speaking of the psalms, I have always been especially fascinated with the words "into your hands I commend my spirit," and this because of these words being quoted on the Cross, and also because so many of God's saints died pronouncing them, if not with their lips, then most certainly in that part of themselves which was on the way of becoming part of His own essential Self.

With this in view, I often looked up the word "commend" in Hebrew but could get no clear conception of its original meaning. The other day, this is what I felt to be the substance of that sacred expression, sacred because of it's being made use of by our Lord. Here is what I got studying the substance of that expression in its Hebraic nature. "Death is God's paying the soul a visit and by means of that visit, taking that soul to Himself." The word "visit" is one of the main connotations the term "commend" has.

I, of course, have no way of knowing what a Hebrew Scripture scholar would say to all this. But I remember reading St. Robert Bellarmine (who taught Hebrew) saying that there are words in the psalms so obscure that we can only guess at their real meaning. The translation I made can be one of these holy kinds of guesses. It in no way violates the Hebrew idiom so it can be holily made.

I don't think we will really understand many things in the book of Psalms as well as in the Song of Songs till we are safe in our Father's House in the life to come, and is not the desire for this understanding one of the chief reasons for the saints wanting to be free from this life and to be with Christ? I am morally certain it is, dear Ronda.

Charlie

Letters of Charles Rich / 87

October 10, 1982

Dear Ronda,

As for thoughts about your coming talk to the five hundred women, I recall a Jesuit Father who taught class here and who is now in heaven. I once asked him why it was that everytime he spoke to the students in church they all paid close attention to him, while when other fathers spoke, they kept moving about in their seats and talking to each other.

What, I asked, was the difference in this matter? And here is what he told me: "When I get up in the pulpit, I am completely myself and speak only from personal experience, while others are afraid to bare their souls to those whom they address."

I have always felt that to be effective in our communication with others along deeply spiritual and prayer lines, we must not be afraid to let others see our inmost self, but to do so requires deep humility of spirit, as no one likes to sort of unclothe their inner self to other human beings with whom they are not intimately united.

I know you are not afraid to bare your inmost self to me, but you have to do the same to others whom you want to bring close to God and this laying bare your inmost self is not easy to make. But it's only when people see us in the same way as God sees us that they become impressed with what we have to say to them in a way that will make God real and vivid in their eyes, and not some far off reality too abstract to perceive.

I don't know if what I just said would be practical in your case. But I remember giving a talk on prayer to some Sacred Heart nuns, and after it was over, one of them came and said this to me: "It's the faith you have that impressed me so much." She meant that it was not so much what I said but the faith behind what I said.

Let those women see the depth of the love you have for Christ. . . that will be of help to them in a spiritual way, and this even though there will always be those who will accuse you of hypocrisy and pretence and a kind of show-off to make them feel you are so much better than they. We have to take the risk of being laughed at for our love of Christ, since He being God, the love for Him cannot be expected to be understood by those who fail to have that love.

St. Augustine told the Christians of his own day that if they would be

88 / *The Holy Dybbuk*

afraid of the laughter of the pagans, they would even be afraid to believe in the Resurrection itself.... Did not the pagans ridicule the faith of the early Christians? There are pagans today who do the same thing, because paganism is not completely stamped out, and it will always exist to some degree and in some form.

It does so in the U.S.A. by the decisions of the Supreme Court as regards abortion, and the religion of secularism being propagated in our public schools in which atheism can be taught but not God's words as they are handed down to us by the Judaeo-Christian tradition....

Charlie

October 12, 1982

Dear Ronda,

...I don't know why, but I am getting more and more dry spells in my prayer life, and this so much so that I can hardly feel myself to be all I was during the first few years in the Church.

St. John of the Cross talks of the need for being detached from supernatural things, like the graces we get from prayer, etc. I guess I am now undergoing this kind of detachment... and yet, in spite of this aridity, I never had such peace of soul in all the years I have been in the Church. Poulain speaks of all this in his chapter on "Trials."

Charlie

October 17, 1982

Dear Ronda,

What a grace it is to be able to pray to God. People consider it a privilege to have a private audience with the Holy Father or with some very important personage like the President of the U.S., yet what is this compared to having a heart-to-heart conversation with our Divine Lord! ...

Charlie

November 1, 1982

Dear Ronda,

...I just came across some words by St. Francis de Sales which

Letters of Charles Rich / 89

consoled me very much.... He says: "We must remember that love has its seat in the heart, and that we can never love our neighbor too much, nor exceed the limits of reason in this affection, provided it dwells in the heart. But as regards the manifestations of this love, we can go wrong by excess, passing beyond the rules of reason." The glorious St. Bernard says that "The measure of loving God is without measure," and that in our love there ought to be no limits, but that we should allow its branches to spread out as far as they possibly can. That which is said of love of God may also be understood to apply to our neighbor, provided, however, that the love of God always keeps the upper hand and holds the first rank.

I was consoled to read these words because I have always followed this principle in my love both for your own dear self and those who are equally dear to me in our Divine Lord.

Charlie

November 3, 1982
Dear Ronda,

...when I get the feeling that I may die as the result of the illnesses that occur, I get kind of scared in the lower part of myself, and this in the same way as all the saints underwent the fear of dying in that part of themselves they inherited from Adam. Does not St. Paul himself say that he did not want to be "unclothed but clothed over," and in which words he gave expression that the lower part of himself did not want to undergo the dissolution of his mortal frame....

Charlie

P.S. Whenever during a spell when I feel quite sick, and know there is always the prospect at my age to die as the result of this feeling, and get kind of scared, I say a Hail Mary and I become as serene-minded as it's possible for anyone to feel this side of heaven, this being a great grace for which I never fail to thank God, and it comes through the intercession of Mary.

With this in view, as regards all the graces from heaven coming to us through the hands and mediation of Mary, why don't more people have a great devotion to her and why don't we hear as much of the devotion to Mary today we once did?

90 / *The Holy Dybbuk*

November 6, 1982

Dear Ronda,

When you get to N.Y. you will have to steel yourself for a big disappointment, because you will find a weak human being in me, full of frailties and faults of every kind, and from which same no human being has ever been freed this side of heaven, including the Apostle to the Gentiles himself when he tells us that "lest the revelations exalt me there was given me a thorn in the flesh, an angel of Satan to buffet me." You can even take the case of David who was holy enough to compose the second half of the book of Psalms.

No, Ronda dear, it's not our strength that prevents us from getting depressed at the sight of our faults and weaknesses, but the strength of Christ, since it's with His strength and not our own that we are strong. "I live, now not I, Christ lives in me." All the saints have repeated these words and the reason so was the fact that apart from Christ they felt themselves to be nothing at all.

What a favor from heaven it is to realize that without Christ we are nothing at all, and that He alone is everything to us—is it not due to this realization that the saints went into an ecstasy of love for the Redeemer of the world? It is, Ronda, and you will realize this to be the case when you see me face to face, for you will then be confronted with a weak human being whose strength is not his own, but that of our Divine Lord.

Why do you think the martyrs laid down their lives so willingly for Christ? Was this not due to the realization that it was Christ in themselves that made them the men and women they were? It's Christ in us that renders us pleasing to our Father in heaven, and not any other thing, so when you get to New York, it's not Charlie Rich you must make a fuss over but the goodness of God, who, for reasons too deep for words, has taken up His abode in the substance of his soul.

...God bless you dear Ronda, and this without any bounds set to that blessing.

Charlie

November 10, 1982

Dear Ronda,

I am reading or rather re-reading St. Augustine whom I have not

Letters of Charles Rich / 91

stopped reading over the past fifty years. What a mind this the greatest of all the Doctors of the Church has! Has he not been called the third founder of Christianity and with what justification!

I carried his *Confessions* in my pocket for years before I became a Catholic and I find his mind to be the most profound in the whole history of Western Civilization.

What Jewish thinkers miss by not having the grace that comes from his writings about Christ! He has also been called the artist of thought. There is no one like St. Augustine to penetrate into the mind of Christ and to write about that penetration with such depth of thought. In him the heart and the mind were never treated apart from each other.

After spending a long time reading him, I recommend myself to him to intercede with God with whom he is now so closely united. . . .

Charlie

December 8, 1982

Dear Ronda,

I know, more than anyone you'll ever meet, that suffering in any form can be a terrible thing not only to bear but to contemplate, but God is always there to assist us with His grace to bear whatever terrible trials He will permit us to go through.

I love you, Ronda, because you are a daughter of the Cross. I do so because of the sufferings you have already gone through and of which same you are still to experience.

God is good not to allow us to see ahead of time all He has in store for us along that line. Tom has often mentioned to me that, had he foreseen all he would have to bear on account of his condition, he'd be too terrified to have said yes to God. Now he has been in the condition he is now in since he was eighteen years old. He is now around sixty. When I met Tom for the first time and he told me of the problem he had, such as temptations to suicide on account of the hopelessness of his condition. . .I said these words to him: "the only solution to the problems of your life is to become a saint." I said this to him because unless he gives himself completely to God, which is all being a saint is, he would not otherwise get the grace to bear what he has to in a

92 / *The Holy Dybbuk*

Christlike way. Later on, when I met his mother, she said that after talking to me he said to her: "I found someone who is going to solve my problems."

...I don't want to depress you with all this talk...but want to assure you that God loves you so much that you cannot have the least notion of it in the present life, and that the only solution to the problems you will always have is to become a saint and remain one until you see God face-to-face in the beatific state.

...I asked my director why suffering is so important and he said because "suffering removes the impediments between the soul and God." St. Maximus the Confessor (600 A.D.) says that suffering washes away the dirt from the soul. ...

Charlie

December 10, 1982

Dear Ronda,

...As for the work in the world not being done if everyone was a mystic, do you realize how deeply externally active all mystics have been, beginning with Moses and St. Paul down to those in our own age? Who achieved more in the world than St. Catherine of Siena who was so involved in the political problems of her own day? And with her we have St. Teresa travelling all over Spain founding convent after convent and having to deal with worldly and commercially-minded real estate men.

You also have a St. Ignatius Loyola busying himself with such mundane affairs as getting the right kind of materials for the colleges to be built. You also have St. Francis Xavier travelling all over the world.... The list of active mystic souls is endless, so don't worry about the work in the world not being accomplished because of the transcendent experiences of mystic souls.

...In the book of Wisdom there is a passage which compares the time we spend on earth as a ship which, after it has passed, the waters do not indicate that it was ever there....

Charlie

Letters of Charles Rich / 93

December 15, 1982

Dear Ronda,

... As to why God hardened the heart of Pharoah [*A question asked by my son.*—Ed.] it's to bring out both the power and mercy of God. It's God's permissive will that's there denoted. God permits evil, St. Augustine says, to bring good out of it. If God did not allow Pharoah's heart to be hardened, He could not show forth his power in overcoming evil. The same is true as regards the sins God allows those who later become saints to fall into.

Where would St. Augustine have been if God did not allow him to fall into the sins prior to his conversion? It's the memory of his sins that caused him to love God so much and to become so humiliated on account of them.

There are great frailties in my own life which I have acquired before my conversion, and they now serve to keep me humble and compassionate with others who have similar frailties. They also remind us we are not yet in heaven and prompt us to want to be there where these frailties will not exist.

The main thing is to love God and not be worried as regards offending Him with our shortcomings. These are as nothing in God's eyes. Does it not say that love covers a multitude of sins? ... Occupy yourself with loving God, for you can never be sufficiently occupied along that line.

When a mother has a child she loves very much, does that mother want that child to worry about anything whatsoever, since the love the mother has will see to it that that child will need nothing which would stand in the way of its happiness. God is like this with you, dear Ronda. The love He has for you will cause Him to take care of everything. You have to keep your precious soul at peace—since it came from Him, it's His property. ...

Charlie

December 15, 1982

Dear Ronda,

... We do need many saints to counteract the immorality so ram-

94 / *The Holy Dybbuk*

pant in the U.S.A. It's not so much the sins of the flesh that matter, but the satanic pride to which the sins of the flesh lead.

I felt tempted to get very depressed tonight and recognized in this temptation Satan in his most naked form. The devil hates peace of mind, so he does all allowed him by God to upset that peace of mind. He, Satan, loves gloom and sadness because we then can't raise up our hearts and minds to the celestial spheres.

On such occasions, we have to call to mind the temporal nature of our earthly existence and take comfort in the fact that being so brief, it can't last, and we will be where nothing will have the power to mar the joy we will then experience. It's only a little while, Our Lord said, the little while this whole earthly existence is.

There isn't much I really have to say. When people climb a high mountain, they tie a rope around each other, so if one falls, the other holds him up. The rope that ties the two of us together is our love for Christ and the hope we have of our one day being in heaven, there and there alone to really enjoy each other's society. So with this holy and joyous thought, let me bid you goodnight.

In Our Divine Lord,

Charlie

December 17, 1982

Dear Ronda,

Friendship grows like a tree or a plant. The longer it lasts the more profound it becomes and the more refined and Christlike. If it does not become Christlike, then the purpose of it has been vain and useless. In fact, everything that happens to us in this life is meant by God to make us more like unto His divine Son—the universe itself has been created for that purpose.

Before I got to sleep last night I was tempted to feel gloomy and depressed. It seems that the closer we get to God the more intimately we participate in the sufferings of His divine Son, something clearly brought out in the lives of the saints, especially those among them favored with mystic graces. If you will turn to the part where Poulain

Letters of Charles Rich / 95

speaks of the "Trials" accompanying mystical graces, you will clearly see the truth of what I just said.

...I sometimes feel scrupulous when I tell someone to become a saint, realizing the sufferings such a person would have to go through. To have gotten to the closeness to God you now have, you had to suffer so much. It's the realization of this that brings tears to my eyes, seeing there is no getting to heaven without suffering of every variety. ...

Charlie

December 23, 1982

Dear Ronda,

You have to be very careful when you read what the saints say about certain matters such as spiritual friendship and what other saints do. You can't imitate anything in particular in a saint's personal life, since the details of that life may not be the same in your case.

The thing to imitate in a saint is his love for Christ, and not the particular way and manner this love finds expression. It differs in different temperaments....

God sometimes gives us a holy person to be a friend who helps us to get to know God better, but the devil is trying to make us scrupulous about such a relationship on account of the good that would follow from it.

I once had a scruple about going to see Sr. Adele Marie as often as I did. My saintly friend to whom I went to confession about the matter said these words to me: "You may need her as much as she does you." ... So you see, harm would have come had I given into the scruple.

When I first went to Fr. Clark, I asked what my attitude should be as far as women friends are concerned, and he said that should be no problem whatever. And when I further asked him if that attitude applied to young women, he said the same thing.

...I myself am a devoted lover of St. Joseph Labre. I don't think there is anyone who has a greater devotion to him. But if I imitated him in his personal life, I would have ended up in spiritual disaster, and I could never live in a Jesuit house going about dressed the way he was and sleeping in hallways in the company of the most degraded people that are found in places he hung around.

96 / *The Holy Dybbuk*

...If you want to be a saint, you must not let yourself become a victim of scrupulosity no matter what the cause of that scrupulosity is, since to become a saint one must have a joyful heart. And do you think the devil, who is the prince of misery, and for this reason loves company, is going to stand by and see the joyfulness of your heart which is pleasing to the God he, the devil, hates with such ferocity? He certainly will not, and so he does all allowed him by God to drag people down to his own miserable state and he does so by making them wretched and miserable as himself.

...When we read anything that a saint says that makes us sad and depressed, it's a sure sign such sadness and depression and fear is not from God, so we must pay no attention to what that saint says along that line. In short, we must pick and choose from the writings of the saints what applies to us and what would help us spiritually and simply disregard everything else they say. Are we not told by St. Paul to "rejoice in the Lord"?

That's enough for one day....

Charlie

December 21, 1982

Dear Ronda,

...God does not want you to follow anyone else's way of becoming a saint, even my own way. We are all different, and God loves variety. So dear, dear soul, give your whole-hearted love to Christ, and be what God wants you to be, you and no one else.

...Some years back, during the reign of Pope Pius X, a group of Americans visited him. After they left, this saint of God said these words: "I love those Americans: they are the bloom of the Church." What a contrast these words of hope and joy [are] to those who think we are another Sodom and Gomorrah.

No, Ronda dear, our Lord and our Lady will not abandon this country and will bring it to God in the long run. For this to be done, much suffering will have to be undergone by its inhabitants but in the long run, perhaps after many in this country will have died for the faith, it will flourish and become a great Catholic nation like other European nations have once been. ...

Charlie

Letters of Charles Rich / 97

December 30, 1982

Dear Ronda,

. . . Why don't more people think of the joys awaiting them in the life to come, since such thoughts would serve to neutralize the troubles of their earthly lot? All throughout the Scriptures, especially in the book of Psalms and the New Testament, we find the thought of heaven's joys alluded to. And yet, what are the thoughts that occupy the minds of most people? Are they not mundane and earthly ones and is it not a shame that this should be the case?

Along these lines, we find St. Francis de Sales saying to the nuns he was directing, "We do not think enough of eternity." As a result of original sin, everything on earth has turned upside down, so that the things we crave most, such as all the sinful pleasures, turn out to become our worst enemies, bringing in their train diseases of every kind. . . .

How free the saints are, free from the false hopes and false values instilled into us from the cradle to the grave. For the believer in Christ one thing alone matters: it consists in looking forward to the day when we shall have the grace to be completely with His gracious Being. Men are false. They live in lies. The values they have end up in six feet of earth. It's for this reason we must shun the crowds who spend their earthly days in pursuit of what is not meant to make them the happy and peaceful human beings it's God's will for them to be.

. . . as to writing you too many letters. . . St. Teresa says that if worldly-minded people form intimate associations to encourage them in their worldly-mindedness, so why should not those who are intimately united to Our Lord form intimate associations to encourage each other in what they hold in common in a spiritual way.

Charlie

January 1983

Dear Ronda,

In view of your letter telling me of the lack of love for the truths of the faith among the students in your class, here is my reaction: I am not distressed when I hear of someone guilty committing all the sins of the

98 / *The Holy Dybbuk*

flesh a human being is able to commit. But when I hear of people not loving the Love Itself Jesus is, that really causes me pain of heart and mind.

There is so little our God wants from us; He only craves the love of our inmost self, so if we give Him this, He is satisfied. It's not great works of virtue God demands of our poor human nature. He knows we are weak and sinful human beings. It's love He craves and this is because of His being Love Itself. Does not St. Augustine say to us, love and do what you will?

The sins of the body have never held much concern with me, for even St. Thomas Aquinas assures us that sins of the body are of less gravity than are the sins of the mind. Men are weak and so it's hard for them to resist the temptation of their bodily make-up. Have not the greatest sinners of the body become the greatest saints, St. Augustine among them? No Ronda, I am not distressed when I hear people commit the sins of the flesh—what breaks my heart is to hear people commit sins of the mind in the form of satanic pride. . . . And so when I hear of the rebellion among Catholics against the authority of the Church, that really causes me to suffer anguish of soul. Did not our Lord lavish His mercy on Mary Magdalen, one of the notorious sinners of her own day, and did not the sins committed by her transfigure her into one of the greatest of all loves of the God-man?

No, Ronda, a thousand times no, I am not distressed at the sight of such a vast amount of physical sin. I am distressed to the point of tears when I hear of someone not loving the Love Itself Christ is, since it's love alone that renders us pleasing to the heart of Christ.

Prior to my entry into the Church, I have myself indulged in the commission of sins of the flesh, but never, never the sins of the mind. I am even now tempted along lines of physical sins, but such temptation in no way causes any upheaval in my inner being, since with God it's love that counts and love only. May God give me the grace never to offend Him in a spiritual and intellectual way, since if He does my immortality is assured. . . .

Charlie

Letters of Charles Rich / 99

February 5, 1983

Dear Ronda,

...You often speak of your intentions of reading St. John of the Cross. But do you realize that it's the sufferings you go through that are preparing you for the extraordinary graces necessary to both read and assimilate all this doctor of mystical theology has to say—and what is it that made him the Church's greatest mystical theologian who ever lived?

The answer is clear and distinct, but to find it out you have to read his writings and do so over and over, because not to read them over and over is the same as not reading them at all, and the trouble is that few people have the time and leisure reading his works require, nor are they willing to go through the terrible sufferings to profit spiritually from those writings.

You'll never really be able to read his writings until, in a mystical way, you are completely dead to yourself, and it takes others to do the killing. I can honestly say that it's through the pain I went through, both before and after entering the Church, that procured me the grace to make the writings of St. John of the Cross the cornerstone and foundation of the kind of prayer life I now have the grace to live.

You have to be dead before you'll get the grace to live completely the life Christ is, so you can say with St. Paul, "I live, now not I, but Christ lives in me." You'll thank [those now taunting you] for making such a life possible for you. . . .

Charlie

February 15, 1983

Dear Ronda,

Tomorrow begins my fiftieth Lent in the Church, so there is so much to thank God along this line.

Referring to the grace of her conversion, St. Elizabeth Seton says: why me? I say the same thing with her: why me, and why you—why have we been chosen over so many other people we know and knew like my own sainted mother. Why did she not have the grace to become a member of the household of the faith? Along this line, though, I feel

100 / *The Holy Dybbuk*

with St. Teresa that the first person I will meet when I get to heaven will be her, since she it was who instilled into my soul a love for God, since as far back as I am able to remember.

Along this line, I always like to recall when I was only around four or five years old, when I was in the women's compartment of the synagogue and I put my head on her lap and I saw the tears from her eyes fall on the pages of her prayer book.

So enormous was the influence she never failed to exert over me spiritually, that when I am asked why I became a Catholic, I am tempted to reply that it was due to my mother's influence over me in a spiritual way.

I once asked her from where she got her deep spiritual outlook, and she told me it was from her father who was a famous Hasid who was known for his love for the poor.

Frederick Ozanam said that that person is fortunate who had a holy mother, and my mother was one of the holiest persons I ever had the good fortune to know and love. . . .

Charlie

February 17, 1983

Dear Ronda,

One of the fathers in the house just informed me that my name came up during a meeting of the members of the house, so that makes me feel that the older I get the more likelihood there is of my one day not being able to live here, and that like Tom, I too may end up in a home for the aged, or the "snake pit" as someone referred to these homes. [*Of course, some Catholic homes for the aged are like retreat houses and are very wonderful, spiritually.*—Ed.]

Yet, when dealing with God we have to be prepared for anything in this life, for once we give ourselves completely to him by unconditional surrender, there is no telling what in His eyes may be more conducive to our eternal well-being. And so, if going to a home will serve that purpose—the one making us more like Christ—so be it. It does not really matter what takes place in this life seeing that, both good or bad, it all has to have an end anyway. Besides, I have already over-stayed my

Letters of Charles Rich / *101*

days in this life and so the rest of the time I am going to be here is really a kind of bonus, and a bonus is not a right, seeing it does not have to be given. . . .

It's easy to say to God "Thy will be done" in words, but it is not so easy to do this by accepting whatever God has in store for us such as a humiliating and languishing illness or any of the different kinds of diseases that can last til one's last breath.

But when we think of Christ and the eternity of the joys laid up for us in the life to come, what are a few moments of anguish and agony to be gone through in this life or whatever humiliations that go with being a human being, and the way that human being has to end up one fine day.

It's to eternity we have to look and not to anything that can take place on this earth, seeing if we don't look forward to the joys of the life to come, what we have to bear in this life can become too much of a burden, driving us to despair. Besides, have we not been told that sufficient is the evil of today and not to become over concerned with what may be in store for us in some future date.

. . . I wrote you at length today concerning the problem getting on in years brings with it. When people get permanently ill here in the house, there are places where to send them. In my case, though, not being a member of the community, they cannot send me to any of their places outside the city. So I have to look forward to being recommended to some place where those without friends are sent when they get permanently ill, because they need all the room in the house for the fathers who teach in class.

The reason I was able to stay here for the 33 years I have been here was due to the fact that I have been able to take care of my physical needs, so as not to burden the fathers here with these needs. But, as I get older, I have to look forward to the time when I won't be able to fend for myself, and that means I have to look forward to going to a home for the aged.

It's remarkable that at the age of 83 I am still able to take care of my own needs, so there is as yet no need for going to a home. But, as I said in the other letter I wrote along this line, to be forewarned is to be forearmed, so it's wise to look forward with anticipation as to what the future may have in store for us.

102 / The Holy Dybbuk

When I first came to Xavier [*a Jesuit high school with a Jesuit residence attached to it* —Ed.] 33 years ago, my prayer was that it may be God's will for me to have the grace of dying in a Jesuit house. I do not pray with too much emphasis along this line, because there is no way of knowing as to what may be of benefit to the eternal well-being of my soul. It may be that it is for my eternal well-being to spend my last earthly days in a home for the aged, so I will let God decide this matter, for the main thing is to get to heaven and it does not matter how we get there.

Well, Ronda dear, this is not the kind of letter I prefer writing. . . .

Charlie

February 25, 1983

Dear Ronda,

What I said about my not being able to stay at Xavier some day was a temptation to concern myself as to what God may have in store for me along that line. It's not God's will for me to concern myself with what the future holds for me, but to live just one day at a time, and leave tomorrow for God to concern Himself with.

Living as I do from day to day, there is always a temptation to worry about the future, and it's definitely not God's will for me. . . .

Charlie

February 28, 1983

Dear Ronda,

A great many years ago, I came across a very beautiful passage in a fourteen hundred page commentary on the Gospel of St. John. It's on the part where the disciples saw Jesus walking on the sea, in Chapter 6:16-21.

I had long since lost track where I made note of this passage, so, in spite of the way I felt about my cold, I went up to the Annex of the Research Library and spent a couple of hours locating this passage. It's so beautiful and consoling that I feel I must share it with you. Here it is:

"For observe that Christ does not appear to those in the boat

Letters of Charles Rich / 103

immediately on their setting sail, nor at the commencement of their danger, but when they are many furlongs off from the land. For not when the condition which harasses us first begins, does the grace of Him who saves visit us, but when the fear is at its height, and the danger now shows itself mighty, and we are found, so to say, in the midst of the waves of afflictions: then unlooked for does Christ appear, and puts away our fear, and will free us from all danger, by His ineffable power changing the dread things into joy, as it were a calm" (Commentary on the Gospel of St. John, by St. Cyril of Alexandria).

Aren't these words beautifully sublime and is it not a grace from heaven to be able to read them? It is, Ronda, that's why I want to share them with you. . . .

Charlie

March 21, 1983

Dear Ronda,

. . . I had an acute experience of aridity last night. It was so bad that it almost brought tears of anguish to my eyes.

The mystical authors all claim that such periods are enormous graces from God, though they are among the most terrible to bear. You feel as if life has no meaning at all and that there is nothing in this world worth living for—all feeling for God is gone and it seems as if we are without any souls. It's hard to talk about this in words—it does not last too long because it if did we could not bear the terrible inward emptiness. . . .

Charlie

March 26, 1983

Dear Ronda,

. . . the saints themselves concluding that because they are weak and frail, more weak and more frail than the average good Catholic, they think they are not pleasing to God, and so they are not entitled to be called saints. Along this line, don't we find St. Francis of Assisi saying that the reason God chose him was due to the fact He could find no one in Assisi weaker than himself?

104 / *The Holy Dybbuk*

Have you ever read a really critical and scholarly life of a saint without the realization coming over you how terribly weak and frail that saint was? In popular lives of the saints these weaknesses are omitted so Catholics get a totally false idea of what a saint is meant to be.

. . . Are we not told in the book of Ezekiel that God will cast our sins into the ocean? And don't we find our Lord complaining to St. Jerome because this saint did not yet give Him everything? "You have not yet given me your sins," are the words used by Christ to address St. Jerome.

No, it's not our virtues that make us pleasing to God, nor is it our faults and frailties that make us displeasing to Him. We are saints not because we are more perfect than others who are not saints. We are saints because we love, as is the case of St. Mary Magdalen. Here we have a notorious public sinner who was infinitely more beloved by Christ than were all the virtuous people around Him. . . .

Charlie

April 4, 1983

Dear Ronda,

With St. John Eudes, I have always felt that devotion to Mary is the same as devotion to Jesus and that they are two aspects of the same mystery of God's love for the human race. Hasn't someone said that God is more of a Mother to us than a Father? Is He not both in one?

Anyway, as far as I am concerned, every time I pay a visit to the Blessed Sacrament, I realize I owe it to Mary to have the grace to make such a visit, and that without the devotion I have to her I would not have the grace to spend so much time praying before the Blessed Sacrament.

There are times when I face a crisis, and when this happens, I feel it's not enough to recommend myself to God, but it's also God's will to spend a few moments at the statue of the Blessed Virgin and to ask for the grace to bear what I have to. This is especially the case of the evening before going to the eye clinic at St. Vincent's to check the eyes. I had four operations, two on each eye, and so when my appointment for the following day arrives, I go to the statue of the Blessed Virgin in

Letters of Charles Rich / 105

our students' chapel and ask her help to bear the decision the doctors would come to.

I don't specify anything I say to her because I have no way of knowing what God's will will be in this matter. I just turn to her and, when I do so, I get a deep peace in my soul knowing with her help everything will be what God wants it to be—I am at peace. I don't think I'd have this peace if I did not pray at the foot of the statue every night when I have to go to the clinic the following day.

. . . for the first few months I was in the Church, I did nothing but pray to Mary, and I did so with a great deal of weeping. I felt that my tears were the only way I could express my gratitude to God for the gift of faith, and I felt it's to Mary I should go to get to God. . . . It was only after several months of this exclusive devotion to Mary, I got the grace to go to the altar where the Blessed Sacrament was kept and spent time praying to our Hidden Lord. . . .

Charlie

April 23, 1983

Dear Ronda,

It's wonderful to see you steep yourself so thoroughly and so deeply in the writings of St. Gertrude the Great.

In reading the biography of St. Teresa of Avila, I was struck by the insistence she makes on the need for spiritual friendship on the part of those who have been raised to a high degree of prayer. She says it did her a lot of harm not to have someone to talk over the experiences she received from God along lines of extraordinary prayer. "A great evil it was," she says, "for the soul to be alone. It seemed to me that if I had someone to talk this over with it would have helped.

"For this reason I would counsel those who practice prayer. . . at least in the beginning, to have friendship and association with other persons having the same interest. I don't think it is possible for a person [who is] beginning truly to love and serve God [to not] talk with someone about his joys and trials, which all who practice prayer undergo.

". . . spiritual friendship is so extremely important since it [the

106 / *The Holy Dybbuk*

soul] has so many opponents and friends to incite it to evil.

"There is such sluggishness in matters having to do with service of God that it is necessary for those who serve Him to become shields to one another that they might advance."

I am not at all surprised to hear St. Teresa say this, because I have always felt a deep need to talk over my own experiences along high degrees of prayer with others. It is for this same reason I go over to see Tom so often, because the both of us need each other to be of help in advancing along lines of extraordinary prayer. . . .

Charlie

May 19, 1983

Dear Ronda,

I am suffering a great deal from tedium of late. I can't pray, I can't read. The only way I am united with God is by my will. It's the last stage of the spiritual life, and nearly all the saints went through it before they went to heaven. It's a dangerous time because God withholds all His consolations and it's very detaching.

St. John of the Cross speaks of being detached from supernatural favors because while we experience them, we are tempted to want to remain in this life because of the joy these supernatural favors bring with them. However, it's God Himself in His essential self we have to have, and this we cannot have in the present life, so God teaches us this by withholding consolations from us.

It's so hard to realize we have not been made for the present life, so we have to have all consolations withdrawn from us to make us realize this.

. . . I got up this morning to go to the library to copy out some of the beautiful thoughts from St. Catherine of Genoa, which Von Hugel gathered together in his two volume work on this saint. But after reading your letter this morning stating the pain is still with you [*I had an extremely painful backache which kept me unable to walk for awhile.*—Ed.], I felt you don't need her thoughts because the back pain will give you ones as equally sublime and equally beautiful, but also equally painful, as everything we get from God has to be paid for by the

Letters of Charles Rich / 107

sufferings of body and mind He permits us to go through.

Every now and then I get vivid dreams of those I used to have intimate relationships with while they lived. Last night I dreamt of a priest I knew intimately for fifty years. I was trying to get him on the phone and I woke up realizing he is no longer in this world.

Many years before I even thought of being a Catholic or even a Christian, I had some very beautiful dreams in which angelic figures appeared to me, and when I woke up I was sorrowful I was still in this world and not where the beautiful figures which appeared to be in my dreams are. I think it was by means of these beautiful figures who appeared to me for many years, that God detached my soul from the need for physical and sensual kinds of pleasures. I felt I was in another and infinitely more beautiful world, so the one I was in during my waking state left me unimpressed since there was no proportion with what that world had to offer by way of beauty and the one I ordinarily lived in.

To this day, I get the feeling it was by means of these beautiful dreams God drew me close to Him, and this so many, many years prior to my conversion. . . .

Charlie

May 21, 1983

Teuerer Freund,

[*Charlie's mother worked at the house of a German doctor in Poland as a cook when she was a young woman. As a result, she picked up German and taught it to Charlie, who occasionally writes a German word or two and reads German poetry and prose.*—Ed.]

There has always been a question among spiritual writers as to whether physical pain is more difficult to bear than moral suffering. I myself find them both to be equally difficult to bear, each one having its own kind of anguish.

Prior to my becoming a Catholic, I was not free from physical pain for many years. It began when I was around sixteen. We were very destitute and my father would often have to borrow money for the

108 / *The Holy Dybbuk*

cornbread we used to buy, and on many occasions all we had for dinner was herring and potatoes.

With all this destitution in view, I got a job shovelling snow eight hours a day. One morning I woke up with both my legs swollen. The pain lasted for months. This pain persisted for about twenty years in a moderated form. It was only after I spent two months at sea working as a waiter that I found the pain gone. . . . It was as the result of this experience I felt physical pain to be as hard to bear as moral suffering. I used to get comfort reading of all the prophets had to suffer, like Jeremiah and Isaiah.

Anyway, I feel it was during these years of physical pain I got the grace to get detached from physical pleasures and which same finally led me or disposed me for the grace to receive spiritual consolations and to depend on them for happiness and peace of soul. Physical pain acted as a kind of novitiate preparing my soul for the profession that took place on the day of my baptism. . . .

Charlie

May 25, 1983

Dear Ronda,

I used to think that these letters, not yours to me, but mine to you, could go on as long as I remained in this world, but I am beginning to feel they cannot, and this for the simple reason that it takes effort to write so many of them and this effort causes distraction. And when anything I do causes distraction, I have to stop doing that thing, because distractions have a way of making me physically sick. I get sick because I can't keep myself united with God in the kind of prayer life I have to live. I'll give you an example:

Before coming to Xavier, I lived in the Paulist parish, so they let me use their house library and stay there all hours of the day and night. After being with them for about ten years, the pastor suggested I should move in with them, and all I'd have to do for living there would be to close the church doors at nine o'clock each night.

I did not see any problem along this line, so I moved in with them. Now in those days, I would go downtown to St. Peter's Church on Barclay St. where the Blessed Sacrament was exposed from one to five

Letters of Charles Rich / 109

P.M. and spend on the average about six or seven or even eight hours a day [in prayer].

Now the first day I got there [moved in to the Paulist church] I found I could not get myself absorbed in God (up to that time, my whole prayer life was being absorbed in God), and this for the simple reason that everytime I thought of all God is, the thought of closing the doors of the church came to my mind. So, as much as I tried, I simply could not get rid of the thought that I had to be home to close those doors—that thought becoming a serious distraction to prayer.

So I went to see my director, and after listening to what I had to say to him about the matter, he said, "You can't close those doors."

I went back and told this to the pastor. They had a meeting and concluded there must be something wrong with my type of prayer life and spirituality if I can't close the door in payment for the room and board they give me. They said I'd either have to listen to my Jesuit director or to them. After telling this to my director, he went to his Provincial with my problem and this is how I got to Xavier.

Years ago, I spoke to Fr. Raphael about the problem I have with distractions to prayer. Being a medical man and a psychiatrist, I felt anything he would tell me along this line would be authoritative. He said they have cases like mine in medical annals, that is to say, those who can't do anything at all without getting seriously disturbed when they have to do anything that requires responsiblity. [*This is no longer the case, for Charlie takes up the collection at the parish Mass and serves a five* A.M. *Mass every day without any difficulty.*—Ed.]

Now, to get back to the letters. As I said, I thought they, mine not yours, could go on forever, but I find they cannot. Besides I have already written you enough to communicate to you all I felt God wants me to let you know, so there would be no point to go on writing them, at least with the same frequency, for that would be a cause of distraction, so this can't be done.

In one of your letters you say I have taught you a great deal, but my job is not to *teach* you or to *guide* you. I am not your spiritual Father because for that you need the services of a priest. I am just a dear friend, that's all Ronda, and so for advice you have to go to someone else, that is a qualified director, and you have one already.

110 / *The Holy Dybbuk*

Many years ago, one of the Fathers in the house introduced me to a woman convert from the Episcopalian Church. She was enormously wealthy and about your age. After being with her for about twenty minutes, she said these words to me: "You and I should be friends." The subject we talked about for those twenty minutes was mysticism. She used to go to Rome twice each year for direction along this line by a great Dominican mystical theologian.

After leaving her, I did not see any problem in forming a relationship with her for the purpose of having talks along lines of mystical prayer and mystical theology, but I nevertheless went to see my director and told him I did not see anything wrong in forming a relationship with this person for the purpose just mentioned. But to my great surprise, this, the greatest spiritual director I ever met, said these words to me: "I don't want you to see her anymore." He said, let a priest talk to her about the subject she wants to talk about with me, and needless to say, I followed his advice and never saw this lady again.

You can see from these examples the problems that arise from assuming any kind of responsibility, and while it's not distraction to spend a long time talking with you in person about the things we do, to continue writing about them with the frequency I have been doing can't go on, and this because of the effort involved in such writing and which in turn becomes distracting. I feel I have already written you more than enough to help you through your "novitiate," and so you certainly can't complain.

. . . Well, Ronda, I don't know what you'll think of all this, but I have often wondered how many more letters it would be God's will for me to write you along the lines of those I have written, so it's with this in view, their frequency has to have an end. I'll write you now and then, when I feel I have something worth saying, but not a letter each day as I have been doing for the past year or so, because there is nothing in this world that does not have a limit set to it and this principle holds true as regards the frequency of my letters to you.

As far as your letters to me are concerned, I don't feel this limit applies to them. If there was no effort in writing you so much, I would certainly continue doing so.

With all the love God has put into my inner being for you, dear beautiful soul,

Charlie

Letters of Charles Rich / *111*

P.S. I have been thinking of all I have just written for a few days now, so it is nothing that just came to my mind. I have also had the subject for prayer.

[*Needless to say, the receiving of this letter caused me terrible anguish. At the time, I was still mostly in bed with back pains and I took it as part of some "crucifixion" Christ had laid on me, so I resigned myself meekly, but with dreadful pain.*—Ed.]

May 31, 1983

Dear Ronda,

I am learning something I did not know would take place as I go on living. Years ago, I thought that the writings of master spirits like St. Gregory the Great, St. Bernard, St. Teresa, St. John of the Cross, St. Catherine of Genoa, and St. Francis de Sales would remain a source of consolation to me till I got to heaven where I won't need these writings anymore.

But I find that I have to keep on advancing on the road to eternal happiness, and that all these writings have to be left behind, the re-reading of them still bring much solace, but not the fulfillment I thought they would bring with them.

As I keep getting near the goal God in His essential Self is, I find that my main source of consolation is the reading of the psalms in Hebrew. There is something about the sound of their words which fills the soul with a strength and freshness from heaven. You feel God intimately present and they make Christ's voice in them something startling to listen to.

St. Augustine said he heard the voice of Christ in all the psalms—and this is amazing because he did not read them in Hebrew. It's to the psalms I go for the strength I now need and the joy, the intense joy of heart and mind they bring with them.

Do you know I used to carry the book of Psalms in my pocket when I was only about four or five years old. I could not then understand any of the words in it, but the mere sound of them used to instill something into my soul bringing a joy with that sound.

112 / The Holy Dybbuk

How we should thank God for these wonderful hymns about which Pope Pius XII says the following: "The Holy See wishes to bring us into closer touch with the original Hebrew—their prophetic wealth is remarkable—their dogmatic and moral richness is astonishing."

At the age of thirty-three my Hebrew vocabulary was about one hundred words. I then met a Jesuit Hebrew scholar who said I should study Hebrew, there being a mystical element in that sacred tongue. So I went to see my director and asked if reading the psalms in Hebrew would be a help to the kind of prayer life I lived, and he said yes. I went and bought a Hebrew Lexicon and after a few days threw it into the ash can, so torturous I found the study of Hebrew to be. Later on I bought another lexicon and threw that away as well. But something in me wouldn't let me rest and that was what my director said about reading the psalms in Hebrew being a help to prayer.

Well, it's about thirty years now I have been studying that language and I find that it's a great help to feeling Christ mystically present in these psalms and hearing His voice in them. Beauty is there mixed with devotion into a mystical kind of blend. A single Hebrew word in the psalms contains a complete thought, so when read, one can't go on because it arouses such profound feeling in the soul and ends up in pure contemplation.

With all this thought, I could never stand the writings of Scripture scholars and Hebrew studies. I find that to understand the words of the psalms in Hebrew, one has to pray to the Holy Spirit, and this is something which Hebrew studies don't go out of their way to emphasize and recommend.

My knowledge of Hebrew is completely self-taught, so it's for this reason I feel something very personal and non-scientific as regards my knowledge of Hebrew. St. Jerome was the greatest master of Hebrew of his own day, and when you read what he has to say as regards that language, you feel he got that mastery of it through prayer much more than the lessons he took from a Jewish convert.

With me, Ronda, everything is prayer and if it's not prayer it's for me not worth anything. When I read the psalms in Hebrew, I realize that it's through prayer I will get the grace to understand their profound mystical meaning and in no other way. I have read volumi-

Letters of Charles Rich / 113

nous works on the book of Psalms, but I got nothing out of them because the one who wrote these works did not take a prayerful approach to his study of the Hebrew words in the psalms. Being such a great saint, the Holy Spirit gave St. Augustine an insight into the psalms which they who do not pray do not have. Could not God give St. Augustine the grace to grasp the full content of the Hebrew words without having studied them in a scientific way? You feel He did, because [he wrote] the greatest commentary I have ever read and I have read many of them. It runs into three thousand pages.

To fully realize how precious St. Augustine held the psalms to be, all one has to do is to recall him hanging the seven penitential psalms on the wall beside his bed so as to be able to read them during his last few days on earth.

And what is it our Lord selected to console Himself on His way out of this world? Was it not the psalm with the words, "My God, my God, why hast thou forsaken me"? With this in view, I feel that whatever great things the master saints have written about God, none will ever equal the divinely-inspired songs of the Jewish King David.

Goodby, dear Ronda, before I bore you to death. Keep loving God as overwhelmingly as you do, so as to make up for those who do not love Him. Give Him your whole heart, and He will give you His own whole heart, and having His whole heart you will have heaven on earth with all the joys there awaiting your sweet beautiful soul.

In our sweet Lord,

Charlie

June 8, 1983

Dear Ronda,

Forget all I said about limiting my letters, and write as often as you feel it to be God's will for you to do so, and I'll answer every letter you write if I feel there is that in it which an answer would be of help to you.

About two or three years ago, I noticed a spot under my left eye, so I never consulted anyone about it. But last year when I saw Fr. Raphael—he is the only doctor I see—I told him about it and asked if I

114 / The Holy Dybbuk

should go to the clinic with it. . . . Yesterday though, he took another look at it and said it has become enlarged so I should have a biopsy done on it.

. . . He said when spots like these are enlarged and turn black, it could be a skin cancer, and if not removed could spread in every part of the body, including the brain.

But it may already be too late since it's been many months in the condition it's in and should have been removed months ago had a doctor looked at it. But I kept putting it off because I planned to see Fr. Raphael. So it may be the ticket to heaven I long for so much.

Charlie

July 28, 1983

Dear Ronda,

. . . When God gives us a talent, we have to make use of it for His glory. . . .

I have always felt it's my job to love Christ and be enraptured by the beauty of His being. If other people are enraptured by the beauty of Christ's being because *I* have the grace to be enraptured by it, that's a wonderful thing.

It's God's will for me to let myself be carried away by love for Christ and that's all. I have no vocation along public lines but intense personal ones, the one of being seated at the feet of Christ like Mary and drinking in the drops of His beauty and His love.

You have this vocation also, but added to it you have something else, a public one, like teaching and writing what would be of help to others. So, it's not important whether you like or you don't like the kind of writing you do, what's important is will that kind of writing help others to get to know God better.

I once said you should write like the saints have written, like St. Gertrude, Blessed Angela of Foligno, St. Teresa, and hundreds of others like them. You have carried out my request in the letters you have written, and so it's these that act like a balm to my soul. I'd rather have one single sentence in one of your letters than pages of your other writings, because single sentences contain the essence of all you are,

Letters of Charles Rich / 115

and it's the essence of all you are I love so much and which same does so
much for me in an interior way....

Charlie

August 2, 1983

Dear Ronda,

...When I worked on a passenger liner the motto of the crew on it
was, "another day, another dollar." In the service we offer up to God,
it's another day and another source of grace with which to know and
love Him whom we cannot love too much.

...Some people mistakenly tell us that we should want to stay in
this life so that we may do good in it. But what is all the good we can do
in the present life compared with the good we will be able to do when
we get to heaven? Can we glorify God on earth more than we can do so
in the world to come?

There can be no proportion between the praise we offer to God in
the present life compared with the praise we shall offer him when we
will see Him face to face in the next life. In fact, St. Robert Bellarmine
even tells us that we cannot praise God in the present life, there being
too many impediments to such praise and that as long as we remain in
it, we can only thank Him for His goodness to us. Praise, this Doctor of
the Church tells us, is reserved for heaven where we will be free from
all that now afflicts us so much and constitutes an impediment to such
praise....

As I already told you many times over, if you could now experience
the full extent of our Lord's love for your dear self, you would be unable
to go on living, this experience of God's love for you being too
overwhelming for you to bear so it would force the soul to take leave of
the body. ...

Charlie

October 4, 1983

Dear Ronda,

I can only too well understand and appreciate your being upset by
the views your students say they got from their high school teachers,

116 / *The Holy Dybbuk*

etc., but you can do them a world of good not to impute to them any subjective guilt for holding these views, by asking God for the grace of a mild sort of disposition.

After all they are God's own children and He cares more about them than you do and being what He is, He exercises His mercy in an infinitely greater degree than He does His justice or any of His other attributes.

What people need is love; they get plenty of everything else from those with whom they are brought into intimate relationships.

When I was a teenager, I got some very dangerous moral advice from those who should have given me sound principles along that line, and yet God brought great good out of all mishaps during the most dangerous years of my teenage life. Those students you speak of, getting you upset, may one day be the exact opposite of what they now are and so they need patience. Does not St. John Chrysostom say that we should convert others by the way we live and not by arguments?

It's the way we live that impresses people and not the words we say.

It's your loving heart which will undo the wrong views your students have, so give them this love and give it to them in an unlimited way.

I don't know what you will think of all this. But after being fifty years in the Church and having read every important book that's ever been written about God and the spiritual life and of prayer, I have come to the conclusion that what people want and need in this loveless world is the genuine love of our Christ-like hearts—they don't need our particular views, since views alone have never been able to bring about a radical change in someone's life, whereas love has been able to do so.

You yourself have often told me that I have been of help to you along spiritual lines, but this help was primarily one of loving you in our divine Lord, so what I have done in regards to yourself, that do in regards to your students in class.

I don't believe anyone ever left the Church who had real love in their hearts for our divine Lord. Those who did leave, and there are thousands of them, did so because they really never had true and genuine love in their sad and depressed hearts.

Letters of Charles Rich / *117*

Can you imagine anyone defecting from the faith who was a deeply joyous human being and who loved Christ the way the saints have done?
  . . . Along this line, does not St. Augustine say "love and do what you will." These are mysterious words and I have never been able to figure out exactly what they mean. The closest to doing so was to feel if we really love Christ, we can do nothing to offend Him, love preventing our doing so. . . .

Charlie

October 12, 1983
Dear Ronda,
  . . . Last night I dreamt of looking through two large volumes of deep spiritual writings illustrated with beautiful drawings of Christ on many of its pages. You can imagine how disappointed I was when I woke up and found this to have been a dream.
  Is it possible that in many of our dreams the angels of God give us a foreglimpse of the wonders that await us as soon as we awake from the sleep the present life is? I think it is, because God will go to no end to make us happy now in this life, let alone in the one to come.
  We have a marvelously good and sweet Lord looking out for our every interest both physical and spiritual, and all the graces and favors we now experience are but a slight taste of all that's awaiting us in the next life. Why are so many stingy in their trusting the goodness of God and why do so many go out of their way to suspect Him of His being unfavorable to their every interest and to every detail of their earthly existence?
  God loves generous souls because He Himself is generosity itself. Was it not His generosity that gave us everything we have, both body and soul? . . .

Charlie

October 19, 1983
Dear Ronda,
  One reason you have not heard from me for the past few days is that

118 / *The Holy Dybbuk*

I am carrying out your directive not to write unless I feel it to be God's will for me to do so, and the other is that there was not much to say.

I spent two hours last night re-reading the Life of Cornelia Connelly by Juliana Wadham (Image Books), and as I did so, I was amazed at the amount of anguish she had to suffer.

First, there is her becoming a Catholic just for the sake of pleasing her husband. Later on, when he decided to be a priest, she agreed to enter the Sacred Heart Convent so that he could fulfill the Ecclesiastical requirement for his ordination.

After he was ordained, he began to realize that his ambition to be made a cardinal would never be realized, so he quit the priesthood and returned to his ministerial duties of the church he left to become a Catholic. After awhile, he demanded Cornelia quit the convent and resume their married state. She refused, so he took the case to court (in England) and won. But the case was appealed and during the two years it took to get the case to court again, he found himself heavily in debt and in danger of going to prison, so the case was dropped.

Soon after his defection he began writing bitter tracts against the Church.... Her three children were taken from her and brought up Protestants. Even long after Cornelia had died, her teenaged son never forgave his mother becoming a nun, thus depriving him of her care for him as a mother. He remained bitter all his life.

As you read her life story, you become amazed at the amount of suffering God allows those who love Him to go through. ... some accused Cornelia of utmost cruelty by her not wanting to go back to her apostasized husband, and among these were many Catholic priests, so that she suffered not only from her external enemies outside the Church, but also from those she would have expected sympathy and understanding from, and all this reminding me of the words of St. John Chrysostom in which he says: "Who know what suffering a person might not be reserved to by living longer?"

There are a few things Cornelia Connelly said that left an impression on my life. One of these is in the words: "It is for the glory of God that we should be saints. God wills what is for His glory. Therefore God wills us to be saints. God wills me to be a saint. I will be a saint. Therefore I shall be a saint. Live for Eternity, Eternity, Eternity, Eternity."

Letters of Charles Rich / 119

Another time she said she would be "willing to be ground into powder in order to carry out God's will."

The most beautiful of all that she said is contained in these words before she died. Her biographer says that she "longed for it—death—as a means of enjoying the ecstatic delight of loving God without interruption." . . .

Charlie

December 9, 1983

Dear Ronda,

After reading the profound thoughts of St. Augustine and the other Fathers of the Church as they are pin-pointed in the book I mentioned, *Eros and Agape*, I feel that the only thing that will really give us peace of heart and rest for the soul is to *feel* the truths of faith in the substance of the soul, and to do so in a way in which our whole being is involved.

I often think that if we have Jesus and Mary in the depths of our being, we possess all that we have to have to be the blessed person it's God's will we should be.

God Himself is so inaccessible to our thought that we have to center ourselves around His divine Son and His ever-Virgin Mother Mary. It's Jesus and Mary we need the whole of the day long to love them with everything we are.

Charlie

January 16, 1984

Dear Ronda,

Now, at this minute, would be an ideal time for me to take leave of this life, for I am at this moment ecstatically happy, so joyous, and there exists at present such deep peace in the substance of the soul, which same is in itself a goodly taste of the delight, the inconceivable one awaiting me in the world to come.

So many I know and love are already blessed to now possess what I still long for, so that to die is nothing else but to be born into the everlasting happiness of the life to come.

120 / *The Holy Dybbuk*

. . . I believe and have the grace to do so, that heaven's joys begin on earth and that we get a goodly taste of them while we are in our present mortal state, there being no death for those whose love for our divine Lord is what it is the will of our Father in heaven to be.

. . . we must rejoice we have the grace to be incorporated in a mystical way and blended with Him. . . .

Charlie

February 2, 1984

Dear Ronda,

. . . Yesterday I was in the Chapel over two hours, so I dozed off for a few minutes. I dreamt I was reading a book with the picture of the Blessed Virgin and the Child on one of its pages. It was a strikingly beautiful holy picture, and as I looked at it with admiration and love and pleasure, all of a sudden I felt I was not looking at a picture of the Blessed Virgin and the Child, but it was actually Herself I was looking at, so I became quite overwhelmed with love and gratitude for such a wonderful grace.

Also, as I kept looking at what was no longer a mere picture of the Blessed Virgin, I got the feeling that every single Hail Mary I ever said did some good for a soul, so this made me feel so joyous to know and realize that every one of the unnumbered Hail Mary's I have been saying for so many years did some soul good.

I'll never forget the beauty of the picture in the book which became the Blessed Virgin instead of a mere picture. How good of God to give me so many extraordinary graces as signs of the love He has for my poor weak and unworthy soul. . . .

Charlie

[*Charlie always has the rosary in his hand and prays Hail Mary's during his contemplative prayer as well. He once said that he had been told that the rosary is one of the few oral prayers which is not incompatible with contemplative absorption in God.*—Ed.]

Letters of Charles Rich / *121*

February 4, 1984

Dear Ronda,

[*I mentioned that if he, Charlie, likes to think I am a saint, certainly those in my family don't think so, including my son.*—Ed.]

Please tell your dear sweet beautiful son that no one is a saint until he or she gets to heaven and that he mistakes perfection for sanctity and that when we say someone is a saint, all that we mean thereby is that that person has made holiness and sanctity the goal of their lives and that they live only for the one thing necessary of which Our Lord speaks when He said that "Mary has chosen the best part."

No, Ronda, God in His wisdom does not permit that we attain perfection till we see Him face-to-face in the beatific vision. And so, it's for this reason He will allow all the faults to remain with us till that blessed day.

Did not Adam and Eve fall in Paradise? If we are prone to the sin of pride with all the grave faults we have, what wouldn't that pride be if we did not have these faults. So you'll have to inform Charlie that he will never in this life have the satisfaction of seeing his dear sweet mother without the faults she has.

Along this line, there is a remarkable passage in the writings of St. Gertrude in which the Lord says these words to her: "The faults (it is never stated which these faults were) which appear in Gertrude may rather be called steps in perfection, for it would be almost impossible that human weakness could be preserved from the blasts of vainglory, amidst the abundance of graces which I continually operate in her, if her virtues were not hidden from her eyes under the veils and shadows of apparent defects. Thus, even as the earth produces a richer and more abundant harvest in proportion as the laborer has been careful in manuring it, so the gratitude of Gertrude bears Me richer fruit, the more I make her see her own weakness. It is for this reason that I permit different imperfections in her, for which she is in a state of continual humiliation."

It says in the psalms that the mercy of God is above all His works, and if we did not have grave faults for God to forgive, how would He have an opportunity to manifest His mercy in our regard. Besides, as all the saints maintain, what really saves our souls is the mercy of God,

122 / *The Holy Dybbuk*

and so we have to have faults for the mercy of God to overlook and forgive these faults. Does not the great St. Teresa say that God "gilds" her "faults," so if she had no faults how could God gild them?

When I first read the above words of St. Gertrude, I breathed a sigh of relief when I realized that as long as I shall live I shall never be completely freed from the grave faults I have, and this prevented me from becoming a victim of what theologians call the cancer of the soul: scrupulosity.

Well, Ronda, whatever you do, don't let anything in this life get you down since if you won't...you will one day be numbered among the saints of God, the saints of God who became and were saints precisely because they refused to let anything in this life get them down—"even though He slay me, yet I will love Him," Job says.

Say the same thing Ronda, and you are as good as canonized! I still say you are a real honest-to-goodness saint and this in spite of the grave faults which others will always be allowed by God to see in you and the same will be permitted to be with you until you are where you won't need anymore to be protected from taking pride in the natural and supernatural gifts God has in His goodness and love so freely bestowed on you.

Tell Charlie he is one of the sweetest boys I ever came across but his theology is not yet what it will be with his maturing years and after he will have read all the Fathers and Doctors of the Church....

Charlie

February 10, 1984

Dear Ronda,

...So many are always engaged in the task of doing something for Him and not caressing His feet like Mary. It's more Marys we need in this world because it's much easier to be Marthas, in that the active life has fewer crosses in it than the pure contemplative one, so it's for this reason there are fewer to embrace the cross that goes with being at the feet of Christ and do nothing but listen to His beautiful Voice and drink in all He infuses into our inner being. ...

Charlie

Letters of Charles Rich / 123

February 21, 1984

Dear Ronda,

...I came across some beautiful quotes in one of my books which you will delight in reading:

"Love is the enlargement of the soul."

"If life is loved, let it be sought where it is not ended by death."

"We are only here to carry our sweet Jesus on our tongue, in telling people about Him."

"And what do those who fear death achieve except to die a little later?"

"There will be nothing there but what we love."

"Godliness deflects or blunts the troubles of this life."

"Let us grant that God can do something which we cannot fathom."

"To ask that of God which God alone knows how to give."

"What happiness did He promise save in the resurrection of the dead?"

"Thou sufferest for a time; thou shalt rest forever." ...

Charlie

March 2, 1984

Dear Ronda,

In case you don't hear from me from next Monday on, it will mean that I will have to be hospitalized [*This concerned a cancer of the prostate.*—Ed.], so I'll have to wait resumption of writing to you until I get back to Xavier—if I get back there, since the case is quite serious and the condition is much worse, leaving me weak to a degree I find it hard to be on my feet. Could this mean I'll soon be in heaven to join so many I have known and loved who are already there?

This afternoon I went to the statue of Our Lady to take my case in her hands. Whatever God's will I do and I need her grace to conform my will to that of God's Beloved Son.

Would it not be a nice birthday present to go to heaven on the 22nd of next month—the day I was born April 22.

If I die of this disease, I will ask the Fathers to bury the body in their own place at the Martyr's Shrine. Robert or Mike Sweeney said they will pay all the expenses the shipment there will involve.

124 / *The Holy Dybbuk*

... There is a beautiful line in Milton's *Samson Agonistes* in which Samson is killed and his father says these words: "nothing is here for tears, nothing to wail and knock the breast."

We have been intimately one in the present life, so with God's help we shall be intimately one in the world to come, so intimate, dear Ronda, that it passes the power of the mind to comprehend the least degree of this intimacy.

Pray God be blessed for giving me the grace to love you so much in Himself.

If I die, Robert will let you know.. . .

Charlie

March 5, 1984

Dear Ronda,

I am very sick, so pray I should have the grace to die in a holy and happy way. I'll be 84 next month, so it's time to go to heaven. Is it unreasonable to pray for death at such a late age?

I'll take care of all your holy needs when I will take leave of this life, and this in a way much more satisfying than if I am here on this earth.

...I can't write more, but what good are words of earth anyway when it comes to giving expression to what's in the soul's depth.. . .

Charlie

March 8, 1984

Dear Ronda,

I was just thinking how many foolish things I must have said in the hundreds of letters I have already written you. But St. Teresa said she did not mind saying a "thousand foolish things if among them there would be something which would cause some soul good."

...Does not Pascal say that Christ will agonize until the end of the world and that He will do so in the members of His Mystical Body. You. . . have already suffered so much for the glory of God but you are destined to go on suffering until God will take you to Himself by means of a holy and happy death. . . .

Charlie

Letters of Charles Rich / 125

March 19, 1984

Dear Ronda,

. . . There is a Father here who often goes out of his way to show his contempt for me. He does so in words that are not exactly edifying. Years ago, this would have caused me a lot of moral anguish but today I just say a Hail Mary for him every time he makes these remarks. I guess I'm too close to my eternal home to be worried what someone like him thinks about me. . . .

Charlie

April 2, 1984

Dear Ronda,

. . . I just saw the urologist at St. Vincent's Hospital and he said that any tumor of the prostate after fifty-five is generally considered cancerous, so he wanted a biopsy. But I told him I was 84, so why go out of the way to make use of what in my case would be extraordinary means to prolong my life, and I feel I should leave the whole matter in the hands of God.

The doctor said that if the tumor is not treated, it's going to spread and when I told him I want to go to heaven anyway, he said why not die in a more comfortable way?

Anyway, I said no further treatment, so he accepted this decision on my part.

I did not have to wait for the urologist's view because I knew I had for years had an abnormal condition in this regard.

So you see, I may soon have my wish along this line.

. . . Cancer of the prostate can be very painful, so one needs grace to bear whatever one may have to along this line. Anyway, it's all settled, though the hospital said that if I changed my mind I could make another appointment, which I have no intention of doing.

On my way out of the examination, I thanked the doctor for his patience with my view in this matter, because it does not coincide with his as a medical man. When I mentioned about God taking care of me, he said, "I also believe in God and I can't see why you cannot live another five years by submitting to the kind of treatment necessary in such a case—either surgery or radiation."

126 / *The Holy Dybbuk*

I really haven't much more to say after so many letters, but this news requires your knowledge so you can pray for me.

. . . When I told the doctor I want to go to heaven, I was a little afraid that he would regard this as false spirituality, but there was no other way for me to make myself clear on the supernatural approach along this line. Anyway, he was very nice about the whole thing and kind of disappointed and which same is understandable.

I took this whole matter up with Fr. Raphael a few years ago, and he said I was in no way obliged to go out of my way to make use of extraordinary means and what would be ordinary would in my case be extraordinary. . . .

I know it will make you feel bad, all I just said, but being as close as we are, how can I keep anything like this from you? . . .

Charlie

April 5, 1984

Dear Ronda,

Every now and then I turn to the pages of the book of Psalms to lift up my soul to the divine heights of bliss which they are in who are now in heaven. I have been doing this for the past two days. I think of you in Christ when I read the Psalms because as I do so something ineffable makes itself felt in my inner being for which there can be no name in the present life.

There is more poetic beauty, more wealth of sublimity in one sentence in the book of Psalms than in all the great masterpieces of poetry ever written, and it's certainly fitting it should be so, seeing the Holy Spirit is a better poet than Homer, Dante, Shakespeare, Milton, and Goethe.

. . . When I come across a sentence in the book of Psalms, I find it so rich in mystical doctrine that it sends my soul soaring into the great beyond Jesus is. It's of Jesus the book of Psalms speaks. It's His voice St. Augustine heard in these psalms.

When I am tempted to get depressed in spirit, I turn to these beautiful hymns to take me out of this depression. . . .

Charlie

Letters of Charles Rich / 127

Undated

Dear Ronda,

When St. Gregory the Great tells us that Christ and the Church are one Person, you can also say that the saints and the Church are one mystical person and that without the saints there would be no Church, since without the saints we would not have men and women in the world to exemplify the life of Christ. And does not the Psalmist say: "Woe is me, there are no longer any saints in the world," and what was true in his age is true also today.

When France was in a bad way spiritually, who was it that brought her out of the decayed state she was in? Was it not the Curé of Ars? The same is true today, it's the saints who will do for our age what they have done in the years gone by.

So, Ronda dear, with this in view can you blame me for telling you you should be a saint and that if you are one you should ask for the grace to remain what you are? . . .

Charlie

April 29, 1984

Dear Ronda,

. . . The condition I have can become very painful so I am going to offer the pain connected with this matter for your spiritual well-being and for the spiritual well-being of your dear husband, the sweet beautiful girls and dear sweet Charlie.

. . . I hate talking about my personal problems. I do so because I will need your prayer and your love when the severe pains come as they usually do in cases like this. Will you ask our Lord and our Lady to get me the grace to endure whatever physical pains I will have with the proper spiritual conditions?

I just finished making excerpts from *all* of your letters and bound them in a little book of about one hundred small pages. I shall have recourse to the very beautiful thoughts in it when I feel low in spirit. . . .

Charlie

P.S. . . . St. Margaret Mary said that in the next life God's friends will

128 / *The Holy Dybbuk*

be able to be with each other all they will want to, and that they will not there have to fear being separated from each other, and these are consoling words coming from a saint. . . .

May 10, 1984

Dear Ronda,

I just got home after being with Tom and I feel very desolate. I have been feeling this way for quite awhile and Tom thinks it may be a prelude to death.

I don't know why I feel this way, but there is nothing I can think of to turn to for consolation. I used to get such a joyous feeling calling you to mind, but now even this kind of consolation is taken from me. For I now think, like the rest of us mortals, you are one day going to leave this life, and so there is a limit to the consolation we can get from another human being even though that human being is the saint I am convinced you are.

I sometimes feel that if the desolation was many degrees worse than it is, I would die out of the sheer anguish such desolation brings with it, and Poulain says that during the mystical state, we are sometimes sad without knowing the reason for that sadness.

Anyway, Ronda, pray I should merit the grace this kind of desolation brings with it, and of which same many saints have spoken of having taken place in their lives.

When I came into my room, the first thing I thought of was a poem by Goethe:

Wer nie sein Brot mit tranne hass
Wer nie die kummervolle nacht
auf seinem better weinand sass,
der kennt euch nicht iher himmlischen macht.

I am not sure if I worded this accurately, but from a translation I made of it, it sounds like this:

Who never ate his bread in sorrow,
who never sat on his bed the whole night through,
weeping and waiting for tomorrow,
he knows you not you heavenly powers.

Charlie

Letters of Charles Rich / 129

May 18, 1984

Dear Ronda,

This morning's letter [from you] is a bit too melancholy, so I must have given you an unspiritual and a non-supernatural impression of the desolation I experience, because though it's a desolation, but coming from God, it has to bring with it a mystical kind of joy.

In fact, in all the fifty years I have been in the Church, I have not even for one moment felt that there is not in my inner being a kind of joy and this in the midst of the most intense desolation. For what God sends and what God permits can never be without something of His own ineffable self in it, and that ineffable self of God is a joy that has no bounds set to it.

In short, God is happiness itself. He is joy and delight itself, as well as beauty, sweetness, and love. So it's for this reason nothing that is either willed by Him or allowed by Him can depress the soul.

And while it's hard to speak of this kind of mystical joy and mystical delight God is and which same He infuses into the substance of the soul, that delight is always there in that substance, since if it were not, we could not go on living a deep interior life or bear the trials that are often permitted to overtake us.

...after reading this morning's letter in which you say that even the sight of the ocean's beauty is not enough for you...no, Ronda, nothing on this earth is enough for someone with such a loving heart as you have. It's the infinite alone that can satisfy that loving heart of yours, and so I am not enough for you and you are not enough for me, but we have Christ to make up for this deficiency. And so realizing He makes up for this deficiency...our soul is always in a state of the kind of delight they are in who are now in heaven...and if you turn to the book of Psalms, how frequently you find the words "I will rejoice in the Lord, I will exult in your salvation." That is, I will rejoice and exult in thy Jesus, for as I have already pointed out to you, Salvation is a noun meaning Jesus.

No, Ronda dear, this morning's letter was not supernatural because there was a kind of melancholy in it which is not Christian. A Christian cannot be melancholy in a purely natural way, and if he is melancholy, that melancholy is more joyous to him than all the delights this false

130 / The Holy Dybbuk

and deceptive world has to offer, because Christ and the joy He is, is never for one instant absent in the substance of the soul, and though there is desolation there in that substance, that desolation is suffused with a quality from heaven, rendering that desolation not only bearable, but a mystical delight to experience.

This is a strange kind of letter, because I am trying to say in it what will only be able to be fully understood in the next life. But, there is a need in the soul to speak of what takes place in its inmost part, even if what we try to say has to miss the mark. We live in an imperfect world, so when we try to speak of divine experiences, we have to be satisfied with our doing so in an imperfect way.

When the prophet Jeremiah tried to speak of the things God communicated to him, he said, "Ah, Lord God, I know not how to speak, I am too young" (Jeremiah 1:4). By the words "I am too young," the idea of a "babe" or an "infant" is indicated, signifying that when it comes to speaking of divine things we are in the category of tiny infants.

...Maybe I got you all wrong, but as I read this morning's letter I felt the mood in it is not Christian because it is not joyous, joyousness and Christianity being interchangeable terms.

Write me if you think I have mistaken your view as regards the subject of death and our wanting to go home to God by its blessed and sweet and holy means. Yes, we want to die, but the desire to do so brings with it a delight from heaven, and if such delight is not present in our wanting to die, our wanting to die is not from God, and lacks the supernatural element such a desire should have. ...

Charlie

June 19, 1984

Dear Ronda,

...It's getting closer and closer to the attainment of the goal of my heart's desire which Jesus in the state of glory is. It's getting so close that I have a kind of holy fear.

I think of the awesomeness of finding myself ushered into eternity. I say I am afraid and yet when I think of it, I am not at all afraid but

Letters of Charles Rich / 131

overjoyed at the prospect of meeting God face to face and all that such a meeting implies. . . .

Charlie

June 27, 1984

Dear Ronda,

. . . When Fr. Clark died, I was terrified at the thought that I will no longer be close to his wonderful being. But now that he is in heaven, I feel even closer to him than I felt when he was in this life. The same is true as regards our relationship in Christ, since being in Christ how can the relationship between us be separated by death? It cannot, dear Ronda, and so there should be no cause for fear along this line. For a devout believer in our divine Lord, time and eternity run into each other.

. . . I had a vivid experience this morning in which, in a spiritual way, I saw those I knew on earth and who are now in heaven. They appeared to me in a more vivid way spiritually than if I had seen them with the eyes of the body. Do not the mystics tell us that the saints have five spiritual senses the same as the body has five sensible ones? It's with these senses the soul sees, hears, tastes, and touches spiritual and divine realities.

. . . Out of the goodness of His heart, God gives us a taste on earth of the joys awaiting us in the next life. He does this so that we may get to love Him in a more intimate way. . . .

Some people, including otherwise good and holy persons, deny that there is a connecting link between this life and the next. All such refuse to believe in supernatural and divine realities. They deny the fact that there are five senses of the soul counterparting those of the body. The saints, though, felt fundamentally different along this line. . . . St. Paul said that he heard words which were too unlawful to speak when he was carried up to the third heaven. . . .

"Believe," our Lord said, "and you will see the glory of God," seeing that He does not hide His secrets from us. He manifests Himself to us in a way too marvelously sweet for thought or words. With this in view, the munificence of God's gifts to us, shall we be content to

132 / The Holy Dybbuk

remain in the lowlands of time? We must not be afraid to ask God for great things, seeing we in this way honor Him most. . . .

Charlie

June 28, 1984

Dear Ronda,

In the last scene of the *Dybbuk*, on stage there are two shrouded figures as they depart from this world. These two shrouded figures symbolize the soul of Chanon and Leah, whose body Chanon, the Dybbuk, invaded. These two souls are now inseparably united.

As I read a translation of this play, I had your soul and my soul in mind and the fusion which, by the grace of God, has already taken place between these two souls.

Like Chanon, the Dybbuk, and Leah into whom he entered, we too have become inseparably united so that in our blessed case eternity has already begun. It has begun by means of the fusion between your soul and mine in Christ the Lord. . . .

Charlie

August 10, 1984

Dear Ronda,

. . . By means of prayer we can in this life partially be what we will completely be in heaven, one in Christ Jesus.

. . . I believe that prayer is a golden chain reaching down from heaven and lifting up the soul to its sublime heights.

. . . They say that people who are in the dark on a strange road sing songs to themselves to allay their fears. I, too—or we too—you and I and every human being now walking this earth, are on this dark road, the valley of the shadow of death, as the Psalmist puts it, so we have to sing songs to ourselves to allay the fears of our mortal lot and the songs we sing are those of eternity.

We sing songs of the kind of happiness that's awaiting us after we leave this world. . . .

Your dear friend in those joys,

Charlie
Alleluia and Amen.

Letters of Charles Rich / 133

P.S. Are not these thoughts beautiful! Are not such beautiful thoughts enough to drive away all depressing thoughts that can come up in this life? And, is it not God's will for us to drive away whatever sadness afflicts the mind?

August 14, 1984

Dear Ronda,

It takes great courage for someone to write the kind of letter I just received from you, because it's terribly humiliating to let someone we love and who loves us know how deeply despondent we can be and how terribly low in spirit we can be permitted to be reduced to by an infinitely loving Lord.

Now you can see why there are so few saints in the world and the reason why most Catholics are content to remain being just good Catholics and not saints. It's a frightening thing to follow Christ during His awful and sorrowful moments.

. . . no one can console someone suspended on the cross of Christ but He who hung upon it. God alone can be your comfort dear Ronda, so that's why I will refrain from saying consoling words to you. You have to undergo the crucifixion of everything that's ever been dear and precious to you. . . .

God did not show any pity to His own divine Son, so He permitted Him to undergo the terrible sufferings He went through. This same loving Lord is now withholding His merciful compassion from you because He wants to place a crown of glory on your head, and there is no way of His doing so save by the terrible darkness and desolation of soul He is allowing you to experience.

There will be more of this before you will find yourself in the house of your Father in heaven. "Ought not Christ to have suffered in order to enter into His glory," Our Lord said to those who were saddened at the thought of the crucifixion.

. . . I could go on this way forever, but what good are words in the bitter way you are now in? Are they not even a kind of insult? So I will leave you in God's hand and it's in that all-powerful hand of His you will find the strength of soul to bear what you are now experiencing.

Charlie

134 / *The Holy Dybbuk*

August 23, 1984

Dear Ronda,

After serving Fr. Musselman's Mass for many years, we have developed a deep personal relationship (he is the Jesuit you interviewed and who likes you very much). Last week I had a problem in prayer, and being that Fr. Beck is many times unavailable, I went to Fr. Musselman with this problem, and to my great surprise he was able to pin-point the solution to it.

So last night when he had a few minutes, I said this to him: "If you were my director and I asked if it's O.K. to have my letters published while I still live, what would you say?" He answered it would be O.K. to do so since the publication of them could help a lot of people spiritually.

The reason for bringing up this matter is that after reading the letters I sent you over twenty years ago, I found nothing in them which would cause any difficulty to having them published during my lifetime, so you don't have to wait till after my death for this purpose.

In fact, Fr. M. is quite enthusiastic about this idea, for he felt the letters would be of great help to people spiritually, and this coming from one I hold in such deep esteem made me change my view of postponing the publication of them until after I die, though at this age, I may easily leave this world anyway.

I also went into detail with Father about the special kind of relationship which God has brought about between us, and he said that such relationships can be productive of a great deal of good spiritually—he said it's definitely God's will for this kind of relationship to exist between us. And though I knew this was so, it was good to have my view of this matter confirmed by such a saintly person as he is. Father has a very good mind and is very practical with a great deal of common sense. If you lived in N.Y., I'd ask you to make him your director.

During the years we have been together, a deep personal relationship has developed between myself and Fr. M. So much so that a few years ago he asked if I would not like to spend a few weeks with him in Canada during his vacation time. I had to turn this down because roughing it in the Canadian outdoors is incompatible with the state of my health.

Letters of Charles Rich / 135

Anyway, I have a real deep friend in Fr. M. and I know you'd be pleased that there is such a person in this house to whom I could confide and whose advice would be of help in bringing peace to my mind. And though this friendship took some time to develop, it's now of a deep and genuine nature.

Charlie

September 7, 1984

Dear Ronda,

. . . You will have to learn how to bear loneliness in a *supernatural* way and how to sanctify the distractions, or to do everything you can to avoid whatever is a hindrance in enabling you to listen to God's voice which comes to you during non-discursive prayer periods. Does it not say "be still and know that I am God," and by stillness is here indicated quietude of soul and non-activity.

I think the biggest problem you have is to ask for the grace to be able to sanctify the loneliness you feel, so that by means of this sanctification you won't get depressed when you find yourself without the kind of activities that you like to be engaged in, such as speaking in public, etc. And while these activities are good, the ability to sanctify our being alone with the Alone God is, is infinitely more important.

If a person wants to get close to God, he or she has to make up his or her mind to be able to be alone without giving into depression by *having* to be alone. Prayer, if it's of any value, has to be the kind that strengthens us to be by ourselves with nothing to do all the time we are by ourselves—how much by Himself our Lord was during His thirty years before His public life.

It's when we are alone all by ourselves we get the grace to get close to God and not when we are in the company of those we feel need our help. And though it's good to be with those we feel need our help, it's more pleasing to God when we ask for the grace to put up with the tedium and monotony of our lives and of which tedium and monotony any life that's any good has to be filled with.

The test of loving God is when we are willing to be all by ourselves without anything particular to do from which we derive satisfaction,

136 / The Holy Dybbuk

and offer up that loneliness, realizing it's then, when we find ourselves without anything worthwhile to do, that's a test of our love for God. We have to be careful not to become God's fair-weather friends, since it's in darkness and desolation *supernaturally borne* our love for Christ is proven.

It's all right to be involved in activities when God's will is entailed in them. But there come many periods in our lives when it's God's permissive will we should find ourselves thrown back on ourselves with nothing that gives us any satisfaction to do. [*These words seem like a sort of prophecy, because, at the time, I was enjoying to the hilt the activism of the Catholic TV station I was working at, but this suddenly was terminated and I now find myself with hours and hours available for prayer and quiet.*—Ed.]

I once complained to Fr. Clark that I found myself too much alone and he said, "the monks in the desert were alone." If we can't be alone by ourselves without getting tempted to be depressed and giving into such temptation, then there is something deeply amiss with our prayer life, for it's by means of prayer we get the grace to bear being alone which is profitable to our soul's progress.

I guess that's about enough preaching for one day. Pray for the grace to bear the loneliness and monotony and tedium of your everyday life, since it's by thus bearing them you please God most.

. . . I too feel myself getting depressed when I am confronted with the tedium and monotony with which any life pleasing to God has to be filled. But during such times I feel God is putting me to the test to see how deep my love for Him is. And so I say a Hail Mary to get the grace to bear such times without giving in to the temptation to get depressed and low in spirit. Remember the words of Job: "Life of man upon earth is a warfare." And being a warfare, we have to make use of the arms with which to combat the enemies of our soul, and which arms prayer and mortification are.

By prayer I mean the acceptance of God's will in everything which is either willed or permitted to take place in our lives. Prayer does not consist in having holy thoughts and repeating holy words, though these have their place in prayer by exciting our love for things divine. To me, the essence of prayer is the grace to accomplish God's will in

Letters of Charles Rich / *137*

whatever shape and guise that holy will presents itself to me. There is no other way we can be pleasing to God, and there is no other way of avoiding being deceived in the love we are bidden to have for things divine.

It's so easy to deceive ourselves along lines of prayer, and this especially during the non-discursive kind which God alone can infuse into the soul's substance. But if we are always on the lookout to accomplish God's will in our regard, and this when God's will is not to our own liking, we then know we are not deceived. . . .

Charlie

September 14, 1984

Dear Ronda,

I was in the N.Y. Public Library today reading the letters of Frederick Ozanam and came across something which would be a good epitaph for my tombstone—you are going to be around when I die, so you can see it put on it.

The friends of Ozanam said these words of him: "He inspired us with a taste for the beautiful and sublime." Isn't this a beautiful way to be remembered by those we love? . . .

Charlie

September 30, 1984

Dear Ronda,

I came across the following in the life of St. Elizabeth Seton by J.F. Dirvin, C.M.: "Here we come upon one of the great characteristics of Elizabeth Seton, her devotion to friends. Friendship was to her, as it should be, a sort of sacrament. It was her delight, her support, a sinew of her sanctity. It was *temperamentally* necessary to her. She was no more meant to live and strive alone than man is meant to be a hermit. She humbly admitted it to Eliza Sadler, that summer of 1797, leaving herself open and vulnerable in the process of entire trust: 'You speak of me as independent of you. Do you not know that there is not an hour of my life in which I do not want either the advice or soothings of friendship?' "

138 / *The Holy Dybbuk*

I love the words "soothings of friendship"—they make me think of you and the friendship between us in our divine Lord. How consoling it is to read of the great saints being dependent on another human being for the consolations they have to have in order to properly bear the trials of their earthly lot! In my case, I have never failed to realize such a need, so that's why God sent you along twenty-four blessed years ago.

They say that in the case of St. Augustine, nothing was so important in his life than the friends he gathered around him. Here we have the greatest human being of antiquity and one of the greatest saints who ever lived, going out of his way to cultivate the love and esteem he felt in need of in the friends he had.

And what about Moses in the Old Testament? Was he not sent to Aaron in order to receive from him the courage to face the hard-hearted Egyptian king? . . .

Charlie

P.S. Here is a thought I just read from Fr. Roothan, S.J.: "There is no reason for being too downcast when you perceive your own miseries, even spiritual ones. For these call down on you God's mercy. It would be a calamity for you if you failed to see your own wretchedness and thought you would not need God's mercy." Are not these words made to order for you?

October 7, 1984

Dear Ronda,

. . . Along this line, I remember that years and years before I ever thought of being a Catholic, I used to browse through the bookshelves of the central circultion branch of the N.Y. Public Library on 42nd St., and as I did so, I came across a book with this title: *The Dark Night of the Soul.*

I opened the book and saw the Imprimatur so I put it right back. In those days I was told that books written with an Imprimatur were like poison to the mind. However, the title of the book fascinated me, so the next time I was in the library, I was determined to satisfy my curiosity and this regardless of the risk I was taking to oppose the views of those who taught me.

Letters of Charles Rich / 139

So I opened the pages and kept reading. At first, I got kind of scared and made up my mind to stop reading too many pages. But the second visit to the library I read the entire book and was startled to realize that everything I read in the *Dark Night* reminded me of the painful experiences I had myself undergone. . . .

Charlie

October 9, 1984

Dear Ronda,

. . . As to your saying that you prefer working with older people [at the TV station] that's true. It does give you greater satisfaction because of their maturity. But, Ronda, we are not on this earth for our own good and our own satisfaction, anymore than He whom we have the grace to love so dearly was on earth for His satisfaction.

He came to give, not to get, since as God, what can anything made by Him give Him that He does not have in Himself?

Young people need older ones to set an example and to sow seeds in their souls which will in the years to come fructify in these souls. Young people need to be in the intimate society of those who, as the result of their experience, exemplify the truths of the faith in their own person.

Has not Epictetus said: "There are enough good principles in the world; what we need is men and women to live them." There are enough of good and holy teachings in the Church. We need saints to *live* these teachings, and young people have to see others who live these truths.

So that's why those like your own dear self who have been gifted to live the truth of faith have to be in contact with the young. . . . And it's for this reason your presence among the young at the University can bear so much good. Of course you will have to pay for the good you do them, and this in the same way Christ paid for the good He has done for you.

. . . Where, dear Ronda, where would I today be if I did not spend the first ten years of my boyhood days in the company of the old Hassidic Jews whom I observed *lived* what they talked about. It was the example

140 / *The Holy Dybbuk*

of their lives that left an impression that has never faded from my mind. . . .

Is it not written it's more blessed to give than to receive? It's more blessed to give to those who don't have what we have already received in the way of spiritual and intellectual gifts, and to impart them to those who will only, in the years to come, be in a position to appreciate what we have done for them—just as the tiny infant has to grow up to be able to appreciate all the mother has done for it.

Goodby dear sweet second self, and I hope you don't mind my preachiness. . . .

Charlie

October 10, 1984

Dear Ronda,

I attended the funeral Mass of one of our teachers here of military science. He was profoundly loved by everyone here so we were all saddened by his death.

Of late, I find that everytime I attend a funeral Mass, I feel cheated afterwards. I feel like someone has gone to a place of enjoyment leaving me behind to be deprived of the kind of enjoyment that person went to ahead of me. But it's not long now and I live with the hope I shall soon have the grace to join all those whom I have known and loved so much, and who are responsible for whatever love of God I now have the grace to have, like Fr. Clark, Fr. McFarlane, and so many others who were equally helpful to me. . . .

Charlie

October 31, 1984

Dear Ronda,

I was deeply touched and consoled by reading a copy of some letters I had written you, and to be touched by reading what one has himself written is quite a joyous experience.

They say when St. Alphonsus Ligouri had reached old age, the brother read him some of his own writings without St. Alphonsus

Letters of Charles Rich / 141

realizing this. So after hearing a passage or two read to him, St. Alphonsus said this to the brother: "Who wrote the beautiful things you just read to me?" "You," the brother said to Alphonsus. I felt the same way after reading the letters I sent you and of which copies you sent in the morning's mail.

...the mystery is why so few dispose themselves for the grace which would enable them to always have those joys in view and which same would act like a balm from heaven as regards everything they are asked to go through in this life, seeing it's God's will we should think of the joys awaiting us in the next life as an antidote to all the sufferings we have to go through all the time we find ourselves in the "land of the dead."

St. Augustine said this whole life of ours is the "land of the dead" compared with the Life in Christ awaiting us as soon as the soul separates itself from the body to which it is at present so mysteriously united....

Charlie

November 21, 1984

Dear Ronda,

...[in heaven] all our bodily senses will be there in a transfigured way. There will be speech there, sight, hearing, touch, taste, and all of these causing us ineffable pleasure, and it's all due to God's becoming Man, thus deifying everything connected with our present bodily being....

St. Augustine says that we cannot in this life form an idea of what the glorified body will be like, and it will be glorified; it's a glorification which begins on earth in an obscure and mystical way.

"All my bones have said, you are my God," and by "bones" the substance of our being is indicated.

I think the saints had a mystical experience of our bodies in their glorified state, that's why they had such deep reverence for every living human being. In every living human being, they, in a mystical way, perceived Christ.

...Is it not to this also St. John of the Cross has reference when he

142 / The Holy Dybbuk

says, "let the vision of thy beauty kill me." It's by means of love we are slain by the God of love.

I will die, you will die, but it's by means of love we will both die. We will depart from this life in no other way than by means of the Love Itself Christ is. In our case, death will become an ectasy of love, by means of which love we shall be made one with the Love Itself Christ is.

For in Christ, death is slain. For Him it has been replaced by love, love being the cause of the soul's departure from its earthly habitation. . . .

Charlie

December 7, 1984

Dear Ronda,

I had a remarkable experience at Spencer [*St. Joseph's Trappist Abbey*—Ed.] the first night there. Each night after Compline the last prayer they recite is the Salve Regina. So during this time the stained glass window is lit up.

When I looked at the most beautiful picture of the almost life-sized face of the Blessed Virgin, the thought came to me what a delight it will be to be with her in heaven. When the thought came to me, I was so overwhelmed with joy, that had it been of a more intense degree, I did not see how the soul could remain in the body.

Instead of the stained glass image of the Mother of God, there was a real live person, and in a mystical and ineffable way I felt myself to be with her transported to where she herself is.

I shall never be able to forget the intense delight of that experience. So yesterday, when I spent several hours with Fr. Raphael in his office, I told him about this experience. I felt that if it was an illusory one, being as he is, so well-versed along those lines, he would detect any falsehood about it. Instead, he said it was a great grace from God, so I should be grateful for it.

When I had the experience, there was no doubt in me as to its being a grace from God, but it's also a good thing to get such experiences confirmed by those who are equipped with the necessary qualities to

Letters of Charles Rich / 143

test the genuineness of them and which Fr. Raphael, as a holy monastic and learned in the workings of the human mind, is. What a grace it is to have him for so dear a friend! When I think of all the goodness of God to me, I can see myself dying with gratitude. . . .

Charlie

December 9, 1984

Dear Ronda,

When I was with Fr. Raphael, we talked a great deal about aridity and the temptations it brings with it. He said it was a grace from God purifying and refining my nature so that when I die there won't be anything left along that line to hinder me from the face-to-face vision of God. . . . Compared to the infinite being of God, we are nothing at all. . . .

But why do I write you all this, Ronda? I do so to warn you that before we leave this world we all have to pay the "last farthing" of which the Gospel speaks, and this last "farthing" comprises the aridities and tedium which go with love of God, because to be forewarned is to be forearmed. . . .

I was thinking of all this as I walked along Fifth Ave. and meditated on all we are, body and soul. And as I did so, I got a vision of God's incomprehensibleness so that it made me want to be with God, so that by being with Him in His own essential self, I will know by personal experience what I am and what you are. . . .

Yes, Ronda, we are nothing in the eyes of God, and yet we are at the same time something so ineffably divine, great, and beautiful. . . .

Charlie

December 12, 1984

Dear Ronda,

You'll have to learn one of the hardest lessons there is connected to a life of prayer, and that is not to pay too much attention to what many saints did and said. . . you will have to learn how to walk along lines God indicates in the circumstances of your own life and, as St. Francis

144 / *The Holy Dybbuk*

de Sales says, "there are as many different kinds of sanctities as there are saints."

Many years ago, I lived by myself, so I did not want to bother preparing meals for myself, even though I had a stove and could cook my own meals. Then I read where the Curé of Ars boiled enough potatoes to last him for many days, so he wouldn't have to be distracted cooking. Well, I tried the same thing, so do you know what happened? I was almost poisoned by potato poisoning!

There were other extreme things I tried to do in imitation of what the saints have done. . . .

I can't go into the details of your exterior life, but you will have to adjust everything you do along that line. . . and when in doubt, you are morally obliged to consult your director, since there is nothing so easy as being led astray in trying to live a deep interior life. Does not St. Bernard say that he who is his own director has a fool for his director?
. . .

Charlie

December 16, 1984

Dear Ronda,

. . . I see a big cross being placed on your road to heaven, but you'll be given the grace to bear the enormous weight of that cross. God has only a few friends to help Him. You must not fail Him. With you it will always be eternity that counts and not the few moments we mis-call our present life.

God will ask you to forego the legitimate pleasures people in your state have, and to exchange these pleasures for supernatural ones.

St. Francis de Sales says that there exists a tradition that our Lord said these words: "Be good exchangers." He meant we should exchange temporal pleasures for eternal ones.

. . . In a remarkable passage seldom quoted by admirers of the great St. Teresa, there occur these words: "For how can anyone benefit and share his gifts lavishly if he doesn't understand that he is rich? . . . If a person doesn't have, along with a living faith, some pledge of the love God has for him, he will not desire to be despised and belittled by

Letters of Charles Rich / 145

everyone. . . . Thus these very favors are what awaken faith and strengthen it" (*Life*, p. 75).

I mention all this because you are going to meet people in life who are very close to you and who, for reasons known to God, have not been blessed with the kind of graces, mystical ones, you received. . . they are unable to renounce earthly pleasures to the extent you do, and to love the ones laid up for us in the life to come. . . so don't be taken aback when you don't see unseen good things of Christ being preferred to the ones most people find it impossible, without grace, to do without. In short, such are as little children who have need of the toys men call created good things and which they spend their whole life constructing, such as our city skyscrapers. In the eyes of God they are the toys of little children who mistake themselves for the adults they are meant to be. . . .

Charlie

December 17, 1984

Dear Ronda,

As I told you, I can't follow St. John of the Cross in everything he says and for that matter any other saint either. I just take what fits in and harmonizes with my own kind of prayer life. . . .

And while St. John of the Cross is and will remain the infallible guide of my prayer life, there is another Guide, the Holy Spirit, and it's Him we have to follow. . . because there was never another human being with the exact same problems we have, and so no one but God alone is really able to understand all our needs along spiritual lines. . . .

Charlie

December 19, 1984

Dear Ronda,

Your letter today is very beautiful and it has given me deep joy and consolation—yes, dear Ronda, there is no doubt in my mind that you have been the instrument of God pouring love into me. I needed this love I got from men in the feminine form as well.

146 / *The Holy Dybbuk*

...I must be either nearing or at the end of my earthly pilgrimage, because I can't read even St. John of the Cross anymore. About the only thing I can still read are the psalms in Hebrew and them not for their doctrinal content so much as for their rhythm and music.

It seems that all that is left now is Love alone and no other thing.... No, Ronda dear, there is nothing left anymore but the Word Himself—because words about the Word only serve to distract and weary me.

Why use words when we have the Word Himself in the substance of the soul forming a mystical blend with that substance of ours? ...

Charlie

December 20, 1984

Dear Ronda,

One thing should console you as you get the grace to saturate your soul with the writings of St. John of the Cross, and this is that no power on earth will ever be able to uproot from your heart the love you have the grace to have for Christ the Lord.

No power on earth will ever be able to uproot from your heart the love for God's holy eternity, and the love for divine things will never be able to be replaced by the love for what is merely human....

"Unless you love Me more than your father and mother, sister, brother, friend, you cannot be My disciple," our Lord says to us. No proportion can exist between a love that is finite and one that is infinite.

...Do you realize what a grace it is to love the writings of St. John of the Cross? What religion has given us such a sublime lover as Almighty God? What writer along mystical lines can compare with this giant in that field? ...

Charlie

December 21, 1984

Dear Ronda,

...For God's sake, Ronda, don't let me hear any more such foolish

Letters of Charles Rich / 147

talk as when you ask, "Should I wear drab clothes, eat foods I dislike?" I am surprised someone with such a fine, lucid, and strong mind should even think of such kinds of mortification, since it's the ones God provides in the daily occurrences which are more pleasing to Him. Your whole state in life is a mortification, so use the details of it for that purpose.

The best type of Jesuit commentaries on Ignatian spirituality always stress mortification of the will to be the kind most in harmony with God's will in our regard. The best way to mortify yourself is to become a saint because becoming a saint will give you all the sufferings a person can endure in this life.

...You often wonder why someone like myself should stand in need of the love of your own dear heart. The reason is, Ronda, that as long as we are not yet completely with Christ, we need to be compensated for this inability by having the love of those who love God. ...and we will need it till we are at one with the Love Itself Christ is....

So, till we are both in heaven, let us not cease for one minute to love each other in Him who is Love Itself....

Your dear Charlie

Index

This is not a complete index of all the subjects covered by Charlie Rich's letters. Rather, it's purpose is to provide a guide to some subjects which may be of personal concern or interest to the reader.

Angela of Foligno, Bl., 75, 85.
Anxiety, 33, 43-44, 100-102.
Arts, 27, 70, 79.
Augustine, St., 90-91, 111, 138, 141.

Bellarmine, Robert, St., 62, 73, 115.
Bernard, St., 29-30, 44-45, 89.
Body,
—and soul, 26, 27.
—glorified, 141.

Catherine of Genoa, St., 25, 54, 74, 106.
Charismatics, 59.
Cheerfulness, 26, 49.
Church, 43, 45.
Connelly, Cornelia, 118-119.
Consolations, 14, 19, 79, 80, 81, 106, 133.
Contemplative vocation, 114, 122.
Converting others, 51, 52.
Cyril of Alexandria, 40, 103.

Death, 36, 56, 62, 73, 86, 89, 130, 140.
Depression, 12, 16, 94, 126, 132-133.
de Sales, Francis, St., 7, 73, 88-89, 97.
Desolation, 14, 128, 129.
Detachment, 86, 88.
Devil, 11, 17, 28, 60, 94.
Disloyalty to Church, 50, 67, 83-84.
Dryness, 17, 65, 78, 103, 143.
Dybbuk, 71, 132.

Eternity, 31, 48, 49, 63, 76, 97, 101, 130.
Evil, 93.

Fear, 36, 130.
Francis of Assisi, St., 41.
Friendship, 10, 63, 64, 71, 94, 97, 105, 127-128, 132, 134, 137-138.

Gertrude the Great, St., 68, 105, 121.
Goethe, 26, 29, 43, 47, 75, 76, 128.
Gregory the Great, St., 5, 127.

Heaven, 31, 36, 45, 47, 58, 61, 70, 73, 75, 97, 115, 117, 119-120, 124, 131.
Holy Spirit, 145.
Human nature, 26-27.

Indwelling, 25.

Jerome, St., 28.
Job, 4, 16, 17, 27, 57, 60.
John of the Cross, St., 61, 72, 81, 84, 98, 106, 138, 141, 145, 146.
Joy, 18, 46, 69, 75, 96, 97, 129.

Libermann, Francis, 65.
Loneliness, 74, 135-136.
Love, 8, 29, 32, 39, 67, 74, 93, 98, 116, 123, 146.

Mary, 89, 104, 119, 120, 142.
Monotony, 17, 108, 135-136.
Mortification, 39, 147.
Mothers' influence, 99-100.
Mystical Body, 10, 21, 64, 72.
Mystical union, 30, 78.
Mystics, 76, 92.

Old age, 36, 46, 69, 101.
Ozanam, Frederic, 77, 100, 137.

Pain, 107-108, 127.
Perseverance, 14, 16-17, 19, 81.
Poulain, *Graces of Interior Prayer*, 79, 128.
Prayer, 22, 39, 85, 88, 106, 108-110, 132, 136-137.
Psalms, 12, 19, 28, 33, 86, 111-113, 126.

Letters of Charles Rich / 149

Reading,
—Christian classics, 8, 78, 111.
—Life of Christ, 38-41.
—Literary masterpieces, 27.
—Lives of saints, 9, 35.
Reparation, 54.
Saints, 9, 18, 20, 25, 35, 44, 53, 65, 67, 68, 95, 97, 103-104, 121, 127, 143.
Sanctity, 3-4, 11, 12-13, 19, 65, 67, 69, 81, 83, 121, 147.
Scripture, 38-39, 58, 97.
Scruples, 96, 122.
Seton, Elizabeth, St., 68, 137.
Setting good example, 51-52, 139.
Sickness, 85.
Sin, 98.

Song of Songs, 18, 29-30, 38, 46.
Spiritual director, 23-24, 25, 82, 144.
Spiritual life, 5, 10, 14-16, 30, 73.
States in life, 54, 80, 83, 92, 114, 122, 147.
Suffering, 5, 50, 55, 57, 65, 69, 77, 81, 91, 95, 118-119, 133.
Teresa of Avila, St., 25, 28, 39, 44, 105, 144.
Trials, 5, 6, 11, 13, 16, 18, 73, 84, 88, 144.
Trust, 33, 100-101, 102, 103.
Weaknesses, 20, 44, 53, 90, 95, 103-104, 121.
Will of God, 8, 34, 101, 102.